GEOFFREY R. LILBURNE

A Sense of Place

A CHRISTIAN THEOLOGY OF THE LAND

ABINGDON PRESS
Nashville

A SENSE OF PLACE: A CHRISTIAN THEOLOGY OF THE LAND

This book is printed on acid-free paper.

Lilburne, Geoffrey R., 1943-
    A sense of place : a Christian theology of the land / Geoffrey R. Lilburne.
    p. cm.
    ISBN 0-687-37200-3 (alk. paper)
    1. Land tenure—Religious aspects—Christianity. I. Title.
BR115.L23L55   1989
261.8'362—dc19   89-330
                                                                   CIP

"Time Is Running Out" by Oodgeroo of the Tribe Noonuccal, custodian of the land Minjerribah, from *My People: A Kath Walker Collection,* copyright © 1970, published by Jacaranda Wiley Inc. Reprinted by permission.

"1979 VIII" excerpted from: *Sabbaths,* Copyright © 1987 by Wendell Berry. Published by North Point Press and reprinted by permission.

Poem by C. S. song from *Theology from the Womb of Asia,* copyright © 1986, published by Orbis Books. Reprinted by permission.

"At Cooloola" and "Australia 1970" by Judith Wright from *Collected Poems 1942-70.* © Judith Wright, 1971. Used by permission of Angus & Robertson Publishers.

MANUFACTURED BY THE PARTHENON PRESS AT
NASHVILLE, TENNESSEE, UNITED STATES OF AMERICA

A Sense of Place

CONTENTS

80533

A Sense
of Place

PREFACE

The environment has recently become a fashionable concern. Politicians take it up for the duration of election campaigns, confident that this issue will draw voters—young and old—to the ticket. The drought and extreme heat of the northern summer of 1988 drew many to think in terms of a global warming trend and to consider the "greenhouse effect" and depletion of the ozone layer as more than scientific curiosities; rather, matters of intense personal concern. It seems to be common wisdom that the problem will be solved if we are prepared to spend some money to "clean up the environment" and if we will make some minor adjustments to some of our more wasteful practices. It may be more complicated than that. It may be ourselves that we have to "clean up" before we can tackle the environment. It may be that only an act of economic repentance and conversion on our part—an act that would cut right to the quick of our industrial economy—will be able to effect the salvation of the environment. But this drives us beyond politics to religion, beyond nature to some vision of redemption.

The Christian church has not been in the forefront of those working for greater environmental responsibility. Indeed, several scholars have suggested that the Judeo-Christian tradition is peculiarly to blame for the attitudes that have led us to this point of environmental degradation. While this claim probably cannot be sustained—I suggest that we must look rather to the intellectual conditions which have pushed considerations of place to the periphery of the Western philosophical tradition—still we have to admit that the Christian tradition has spoken ambiguously to this issue, at times fueling the mythology of development, at others aiding the simple celebration of earth's beauty and the call for faithful stewardship. The problem appears to be that while the Hebrew Scriptures speak centrally of the land, its preservation and proper use, this concern is entirely lost in the New Testament. By universalizing the scope of God's reign, the New Testament appears to trivialize the concern with place and locality and to move its spirituality beyond issues of the land. In an attempt to leap over this difficulty many scholars have sponsored a return to theologies of the earth or creation.

It is my conviction that creation and natural theologies which, in effect, bypass the distinctive New Testament faith will not resolve the ambiguity that lies deep within the Christian tradition. Only an engagement with the central christological affirmations of the New Testament can do that and take us to the place where creative Christian options can be discerned. To precisely this task I have directed my efforts in this book. The work offers an extended essay on the foundations and direction of a Christian theology of the land. Rather than survey the broad range of work currently being done in the area, the book presents a theological proposal that engages the biblical theme of redemption and the central New Testament affirmation that "God was in Christ reconciling the world to himself."

The work grew out of a sabbatical spent in Australia in 1985–1986. After fourteen years in the United States the rediscovery of the landscapes of my youth affected me deeply. At the same time, however, I was dismayed to discover the degree to which Australia's delicate ecological balance was being disturbed by the activities of human "development." Clearly, I was not the first to have become concerned about these matters. In Australia, there is a whole company of painters, poets, and novelists who have celebrated the beauty of that unique landscape. Many of these, such as Judith Wright, have been at the forefront of the movement for greater environmental responsibility. As I spoke with agricultural scientists, farmers, and rural clergy, I sensed a need for a theology that would address itself to the emerging problems in the human relationship with the land.

On my return to the United States I found that the rural crisis had deepened, and that many churches and clergy were redefining their ministry to farmers and rural communities in the face of the crisis. In particular, The United Methodist Church was engaged in a process of regional hearings on agriculture and rural life issues. Through my involvement in this process the ideas that had begun to form in Australia about a theology of the land came into sharper focus. For all of us it became clear that just beneath the surface of the rural crisis lurked the more pervasive issue of environmental damage brought about by modern agricultural methods. Could the insights of the Australian experience be pertinent in the North American context?

Part and parcel of my learning in Australia was the rediscovery of the wisdom of the indigenous people of Australia. In hearing the Aboriginal stories and songs about a beloved land, I was struck by the incredible strength of their bond to the land—the vitality of their sense of place. There is almost a total contrast between their ways and ours; on balance they exhibited an ecological wisdom far superior to our own. In sharing the Australian experience with clergy and farmers in the United States, I realized that the unique religion of the Australian Aboriginal people was deeply relevant to the quest for a responsible Christian theology of the land.

In setting this theological essay in an Australian context I do not mean to suggest that these things are going on only in Australia. The points of commonality between the environmental and agricultural crises in Australia and the United

11

PREFACE

States are almost too numerous and too obvious to require comment. There seemed to be an advantage, however, for North American readers to learn of a place far removed from their own in geography and history. Here once again the shock of the new could promote insight that might not arise in a rehash of the familiar. Given the range of similarities, however, insights from the one context could inform the other. In the United States too a chorus of voices cry out for the deliverance of the land from the degradation that modern development—settlement, farming, and mining—is causing throughout the land. In linking up with these various voices, I offer my contribution to the quest for a Christian theology of the land that speaks from the central symbols of Christian faith.

A travel grant from the North American Association of Theological Schools and the generous sabbatical policy of United Theological Seminary made my Australian sabbatical possible. I gratefully acknowledge the very material assistance these two bodies provided for this work. The original version of these ideas was a series of lectures given at the annual theology conference of the West Australian clergy of the Uniting Church in Australia. I gratefully acknowledge the help of Dr. Michael Owen of the Perth Theological Hall in undertaking the initial lectures and of Dr. Veronica Brady of the English Department at the University of Western Australia in relating concerns with the environment to the rich tradition of Australian literature. Rex Matthews has been both editor and friend in the process of reshaping this material for publication. Finally, my wife, Peta, has patiently lived with me and the manuscript during the months of its production and has patiently read and critiqued all I have written. For this labor of love I am more than grateful.

Dayton, Ohio
October 1988

CHAPTER ONE

From the Secular City to a Theology of the Land

In 1980, in a small town called Noonkanbah in the northern region of Western Australia, a conflict over the issue of land occurred between the Aboriginal people and the state government. Land that was sacred to the Aborigines had been found to be rich in oil. To begin drilling for oil, however, would involve the destruction of a religious site of the Aborigines. When groups of whites, many representing Christian churches, joined with the Aborigines in protesting the plan to drill for oil, the state government, under the leadership of Sir Charles Court, decided to step in. Although by this time the AMAX corporation was somewhat reluctant to proceed with the drilling, the state government brought out the army to escort the oil-drilling equipment into the disputed area.

In an event which had about it all the marks of a biblical conflict, the military might of a modern state was sent against a few unarmed Aborigines and concerned white demonstrators. At the level of power there was obviously no contest, just as at the level of values there seemed to be no contact. What lay behind the seeming irreconcilable differences was a clash in understandings of the land: between land as economic resource and land as sacred heritage, between land as commodity and land as repository of religious meaning. In this clash military power assured the immediate triumph of the economic viewpoint. The strength of the moral claim, however, was not so easily settled. The powerless people of religious faith witnessed to the strength of this claim.

There is a striking similarity between this confrontation and that between Ahab and Naboth, recorded in 1 Kings 21.[1] Land that had been in the possession of Naboth's family for generations lay close to King Ahab's palace, prompting Ahab's desire to acquire it. When Naboth refuses to sell the land to the king, Ahab and his wife, Jezebel, have him murdered and claim the land as their own. At the Lord's prompting the prophet Elijah takes up Naboth's cause. A dramatic confrontation ensues. On the one side stand King Ahab and Queen Jezebel, and on the other the prophet Elijah representing the murdered Naboth. The difference in worldly power is total, but Elijah articulates the voice of another power. He announces the crime of Ahab and tells him plainly of the consequences of his act: " 'Have you killed, and also taken possession?' . . . Thus says the Lord, 'In the place where the dogs licked up the blood of Naboth shall dogs lick your own blood ' " (v. 19).

What is at stake in this confrontation is two views of the land. For Ahab the land is a means of wealth, and as such is a tradable commodity. For Naboth this parcel of land is the inheritance of his fathers, and so cannot be sold to another. Even though Naboth used the property as a vineyard, Ahab wished to "develop" and "utilize" the land according to his own plans. Both intended to make use of the land, but one in the context of personal gain and the other in the frame of religious inheritance. The prophet of the Lord endorsed the attitude of Naboth and condemned that of Ahab. If Ahab's superior force guaranteed his immediate victory, it did not protect him from the long-term judgment of the Lord.

Conflicts between tribal peoples and European settlers over issues of land rights have emerged repeatedly in the history of our nations. In North America the disputes continue as Native Americans seek recompense for past wrongs and the basis for future livelihood in traditional lands.[2] Although the might of the states ensures their immediate success, their victories may come to haunt them and us as we face the devastation our possession has introduced. Perhaps we shall need to think more seriously about the judgment of the Lord in our own day.

The issues this book seeks to understand are focused in the incident at Noonkanbah, seen against the backdrop of the biblical parallel of the narrative of Ahab and Naboth. As we face the tragic story of recent environmental degradation, in Australia, the United States, and throughout the world, we need to ask ourselves if we might be able to learn something vital about the care of the earth from the indigenous peoples of our continents. Yet this is an issue that cannot be understood apart from theological reflection. We cannot understand, let alone resolve, the disputed claims to land without digging deeply into the religious heritage of our peoples. We must seriously come to terms with the fundamentally religious viewpoint of the Aborigines, and we must critically examine the historical and theological foundations of our own "secular" view.[3] For all its religious roots, modern secularity in itself provides neither basis for understanding the religiously based claims of indigenous peoples to land nor foundation for adjudication between such diverse views. It is here that the role of religious and theological reflection may be of most value.

The incident at Noonkanbah calls us to sober and disciplined reflection. It stands at the beginning of the decade of the eighties, a decade when the particular problems of the preservation of the environment and the equitable distribution of land came to haunt us. Yet Noonkanbah cannot be understood without reference to the sixties, the decade of which the mood of progress and development the incident expresses were characteristic. Thus, the eighties as the decade of land crisis and the sixties as the decade of secularity are both pertinent to our theme.

A SENSE OF PLACE

1. CRISIS ON THE LAND IN THE EIGHTIES

Few things in contemporary experience speak more eloquently of the environmental problem than the North American rural crisis of the mid to late eighties. In 1985 more than 43,000 farms in the United States failed, and the U.S. Department of Agriculture estimated at that time that of the nation's 630,000 full-time farmers, fully a third were in danger of financial collapse.[4] While the number of farm failures fell in the two following years because of the new farm credit legislation, it is likely that massive farm failures will occur in the coming years. Of course, the problem does not stop there. Because of the so-called ripple effect, unemployment and business failure follow the departure of families from farms. A 3.6 percent rate of farm failure estimated in 1985 meant that the economy had to create another 112,000 jobs for the farmers and rural small business people who went out of business in this single year.[5]

This massive social upheaval has been compared to the movement in Europe in the fifteenth century in which the old three-field system of agriculture with its common lands for grazing was broken up by the movement to enclose the land owned by wealthy persons. Just as this major change in the patterns of land distribution upset a social balance that had emerged over the centuries of feudal agriculture, so our patterns of land ownership are changing, again resulting in social upheaval. It has been estimated that if 19 percent of the farm families in the United States are eliminated in this crisis, then the ripple effect will displace some 6.4 million persons. Outmigration from rural areas already topped the one million mark in the year 1986/87, with signs of much more to come.

The cry has gone up in a variety of quarters that the family farm is disappearing. Figures bear out the claim that a massive shift of land ownership is occurring in the United States, from small and mid-size operators to large corporations. If present trends continue, the family farm will be replaced by giant corporate agribusinesses. This has more

16

than sentimental consequences, for it points to a fundamental structural change in the patterns of North American agriculture, a change that contributes to the mounting ecological damage to the croplands of the world.

The plight of black farmers emphasizes the structural character of this change in land ownership, for they have been especially hard hit. In the year 1910 black land ownership in the United States amounted to fifteen million acres, and blacks were operating 910,000 farms. In 1978 the number of black farm operators had been reduced to 57,000 with control of access to 4.2 million acres. Shantilal Bhagat remarks, "At this rate of decline there will be no Black farmers in the U.S. twenty years from now."[6]

The change from the small or mid-size family farm to the megafarms is not the result of inevitable economic pressures, nor is it the result of inefficiency, as is frequently claimed. In fact, Department of Agriculture research amply illustrates that in terms of efficiency the small family farm represents an optimum. Government policy relating to the tax structure and the payment of farm subsidies is the cause. A recent writer remarks:

> Megafarms make money through investment, not by growing things. The tax code makes their investments profitable, and the practice of subsidizing every bushel of a given commodity at the same rate, no matter what the volume, gives megafarms the final edge to beat out competitors on family farms.[7]

Beyond that there are the broader issues of the quality of the foods being produced, the long-term costs of their present mode of production, and the quality of life being established.

There is some irony in the fact that the Latin American policies of both Democrat and Republican administrations in the United States reflect the policies governing the domestic rural society. As William Sloane Coffin has noted, foreign policies reflect domestic policies in this matter.[8] In

17

both cases the government is, in effect, taking land out of the hands of the people and transferring it to the hands of corporations. We must face the question: Is this the sort of change in social fabric that we want for our countries? And where in the world do we find effective land reform? Only in communist countries, such as Nicaragua, it seems, are there sustained attempts to return land to small farmers who will care for it and live by it.

Countless examples of this pattern of land redistribution on a global scale could be listed. Perhaps nothing brings the plight of Third World peoples closer to home than the plight of the former landed peoples whom our European cultures has dispossessed. In particular, I would like to focus on the experience of the Australian Aborigine. Aboriginal poet Kath Walker describes the prospects of her people in these frank terms: "My people face dispossession, disease and death . . . . the future is grim. Let us not forget, however, that this makes the future grim for all Australians."[9] Walker goes on to speak of the multitude of problems from which Aboriginal society suffers, including poverty; infant mortality; unemployment; and lack of education, power, authority, and influence. But what lies at the heart of these problems is the issue of land, for tribal lands with their sacred sites form the backbone of the Aboriginal religion and culture. Dispossession from these lands, followed by their desecration through mining and grazing, is at the heart of the Aboriginal's cultural disempowerment and degradation.

The global pattern of redistribution of land control and the transition to a monocultural form of agriculture goes hand in hand with the increased use of chemical fertilizers. When combined with the changeover to corporate ownership and management of the land, these transitions have accelerated already stunning rates of soil degradation and conversion of farm land. On a global scale human agriculture is estimated to have destroyed 430 million hectares of crop and grazing land since agriculture emerged 7,500 years ago. The Worldwatch paper on soil erosion reports that the 3.1 billion hectares of total world cropland are presently being lost through soil erosion at the rate of 7 percent every decade.[10]

This global problem is strikingly apparent in Australia, where for each man, woman, and child in the present population 11.2 hectares of cropland have been destroyed permanently in the last 200 years. Of the mere 10 percent of Australian land suitable for agriculture, the so-called heartlands, already 25 percent is lost forever, due to the effects of soil erosion.[11] Further, a stunning 51 percent of agricultural and pastoral land in Australia is in need of some form of soil conservation treatment.

The figures for the United States, though better than those for Australia, are no cause for complacency. In this country 3.5 hectares of cropland have been destroyed for each man, woman, and child. It is assumed that soil depletion occurs if erosion exceeds five tons per acre per year. Yet on 169 million acres of the best U.S. farmland annual loss runs at 23.2 tons per acre.[12]

When the figures for soil erosion are combined with figures for conversion of farmland to other uses, a fuller picture of the loss of farmland emerges. Present conservative estimates state that at least three million acres of farmland are lost annually through conversion to other uses, roads, subdivisions, and shopping malls. This translates into the loss of four square miles of prime farmland every day.[13]

To be sure, there are some encouraging signs. Between March 1986 and February 1988 the Conservation Reserve Program was able to convert 10.68 million hectares of highly erodible United States cropland to grassland and woodland.[14] However, following the greatly reduced harvest of the 1988 drought year there is pressure to return these lands to cropping. Further, the diminishing growth in global grain production from 1984 onward and the possibility of global food shortages will produce increasing pressure to return these converted lands to cropping.

The ongoing rural crisis is bound up with this massive shift in land ownership. While the megafarm has been able in some cases to increase grain production, this has not always been achieved in environmentally sound ways. Whereas individual farm families often had concern to safeguard the land so that they might pass it on to their children and their children's children, corporations rarely have such long-term commitments. It is usually more "profitable" to farm a property to the point of its maximum production—that is, to the point of its soil's exhaustion—and then to sell and move on.

Wendell Berry has remarked that in attitudes to the land there are two groups, the exploiters and the nurturers. While there may be many good people caught in the middle, this typology is useful in highlighting the different attitudes that war with one another in our society and, often, within the hearts of hard-pressed farmers. Many who care deeply for the future of their land are forced to resort to heavy use of chemical fertilizers and pesticides to secure sufficient return to keep up loan payments.

There is deep irony in the fact that in the history of our lands nurturing models of land use predominated. In Berry's terms the Australian Aborigines, like the North American Indians, were nurturers. Their attitudes grew out of a religious understanding in which the land was held in sacred trust and preserved for future generations. As a result of the European settlements that future is no longer theirs, and we, the masters of the new future, must now critically examine the exploiting attitudes which have brought us to the brink of environmental disaster. In contrast to the religious understanding of the indigenous people, our secular view of reality has authorized the unbridled exploitation of the environment for immediate economic gain. As a means of understanding the spirit and the theological foundations of this secular view, a brief return to the sixties will be valuable.

2. THE SIXTIES AND THE SECULAR CITY

In the splendid era of the sixties we seemed poised on the verge of magnificent achievements. The almost magical powers of a gleaming new technology were pointed at the moon, and the vast riches of the North American continent were being positioned for sustained and effective onslaught on poverty and underprivilege throughout U.S. society. The future was surely bright for a nation looking through the telescope of time to the decades ahead.

In Australia too there was an era of optimism and problem solving. Kath Walker describes her experience of the sixties: "I feel the sixties as a decade was optimistic. I think it was a feeling that affected many levels of the Australian society. People felt that if we, the Aborigines, could survive, then together we could all build something fine for everyone." I remember well those feelings, for I shared them as a young theological student in Melbourne, Australia. In the late sixties Melbourne was a hotbed of ideas and movements. Whether one was concerned for peace—Australians were fighting and dying alongside U.S. soldiers in Vietnam— rights for Aborigines, or any number of other environmental, political, or cultural concerns, it seemed that the overriding necessity was to rid the nation of the conservative and unimaginative government of the Liberal Party.

At Melbourne University, in the theological halls of Queens', Ormond, and Trinity Colleges, we were caught up in the ferment of the times. The issue of the Vietnam war was central in our thinking, but so were the issues of life in the cities. Melbourne was experiencing the stresses of population growth as migrants from Europe and Northern Africa were steadily increasing the work force and the demand for housing. Dealing with this increasing cultural diversity and the stresses of life in high-rise apartment blocks seemed to be part of the rhythm of life for inner-city congregations such as the Church of All Nations in the Melbourne suburb of Carlton. Political involvement, peace activism, and responding to the social problems of urban living seemed to us fully in line with the new theology we were learning. It seems to me that the work that best sums up the spirit of that age was Harvey Cox's *Secular City*.

Published in 1965, *The Secular City: Secularization and Urbanization in Theological Perspective* was a brilliant

21

synthesis of sociological, historical, and theological analysis. The book argued for a new understanding of the style and substance of theology, in which theology would no longer be indifferent to its physical and cultural context. Claiming that our theology up to that time had implicitly been a town theology, Cox issued the challenge to develop an explicit theology of the "technopolis." He challenged Christians to accept the city for what it was, not a godless evil to be resisted or fled but the outgrowth of a historical process that was rooted in the faith we profess. The newfound mobility and anonymity of the urban centers opened up an arena for Christian freedom and responsibility. Theology needed to take heed of this transition and to reflect in its style and substance the reality of the modern urban setting.

Secularization was the social force which has brought about the age of the technopolis, and by this Cox meant the process whereby society has been delivered from the control of religion and metaphysics. It was a force released in many fundamental ways by the Old Testament understandings of God and God's dealing with Israel. Cox saw in secularization three interrelated aspects: the disenchantment of nature, the desacralization of politics, and the deconsecration of values, each of which he traced back to the Hebrew Scriptures.

Thus Cox traces the *disenchantment of nature* back to the Genesis account of creation, which separates God from nature: nature is God's creation, but God has his life apart from creation. Further, it separates human person from nature: as the image of God humanity is given specific responsibilities vis-à-vis the natural order. Nature is not semidivine, as in magical belief, nor is it sacred; thus, humans can perceive it in a matter-of-fact way. The secular view stands in sharp contrast to that which preceded it. "Presecular man lives in an enchanted forest. Its glens and groves swarm with spirits. Its rocks and streams are alive with friendly or fiendish demons. Reality is charged with magical power that erupts here and there to threaten or benefit man."[15]

In this world view nature is to be treated with utmost respect, not studied objectively, manipulated, or experimented with. Disenchantment is the process in which persons come no longer to regard nature as sacred, and it offers the liberation to study nature objectively, to use experimental methods to test learnings, and to try new ways of manipulating nature. The disenchantment of nature provides "an absolute precondition for the development of natural science."[16]

Similarly, biblical faith pushes toward the *desacralization of politics*. In the exodus event God challenges the rule of a legitimately constituted monarch, the pharaoh of Egypt, and biblical history often ranges God with the forces of change and transformation in human history. Yahweh emerges as a God of history, so that history becomes the arena for God's free activity. Released from cyclical patterns history is opened to the wider possibilities for political and social change. In turn this has consequences for faith. If God is concerned with social and political matters, then faith is no longer acquiescence to the eternal round, the status quo, but becomes the active search for the will of God and the active engagement in history to realize that will.

Finally, the *deconsecration of values* is grounded in the Old Testament, specifically the rejection of idolatry in the Sinai covenant. Because of the absolute difference of Yahweh from all human products, all human values are relativized. This argument, without further discussion of the Enlightenment and the discovery of historical method, appears a little tendentious, but we will certainly admit that this deconsecration of values is an intimate accessory of secularization.

In the conjunction of these three processes, science, politics, and ethics are freed from the rule of magic: each is constituted as an independent area of thought and inquiry that cannot be reduced to branches of religion. Cox is ready to admit that secularization can have negative or evil sides, for freedom may be used negatively and irresponsibly. However, the emergence of this possibility was by no means

23

necessary, and in effect it was improbable. The opportunities of our freedom stretched out before us; all we needed was the faith and courage to grasp our God-given freedom. What followed was a call to active Christian involvement in the political processes of the secular state, an end to Christian withdrawal, and a willingness to take the risks and challenges that our historical freedom opened up for us.

Yet how quickly times change! At the end of the eighties we are faced with the tale of massive environmental degradation, which seems to have been fueled by the very enthusiasm of movements of secularization. Within just a few years of the publication of *The Secular City* another scholar was finding in the very same developments outlined by Cox "the historical roots of our ecological crisis." In a widely acclaimed essay Lynn White, Jr. pointed to the Judeo-Christian faith as providing the roots of the crisis we now face.[17] The early Genesis teaching that humanity is made in God's image, the argument claims, sets humanity apart from nature and thus invites the notion that the physical creation was created for human benefit and human rule.

White's work has obvious parallels with that of Cox, but the difference is striking. Cox sees secularization as opening for us an arena for freedom and responsibility; White sees that, free of religious constraints, we abuse our freedom in ways that are destructive of the natural environment. Our exercise of seemingly unlimited freedom has quickly brought us up against some very real limits in the environment. For the first time we are coming to see our nation, our world, as "a place of limited resources, finely balanced."[18] In many ways White's view sets the context in which we may understand the more recent work of Walter Brueggemann.

3. RETURN TO THE LAND

A book which is in many ways prophetic of the issues we face in the nineties is Walter Brueggemann's *The Land: Place as Gift, Promise, and Challenge in Biblical Faith*. Published in 1977, Brueggemann's work differs sharply from Cox's.

There is a central shift of setting from the city to the land. While this move in some ways reflects Brueggemann's personal experience of farm life, fundamentally it represents another reading of the situation of modern life. What is at stake, I suggest, is an alternate reading of the movements of history and the challenge of faith, both in the biblical context and in our own contemporary setting. Let me single out three areas for contrast and comparison between these two works.

1. Like Cox, Brueggemann places his focus on the Hebrew Scriptures, yet here the emphasis is different. According to Brueggemann, "Land is a central, if not *the central theme* of biblical faith."[19] Not denying the importance of history and the historicity of Israel's understanding of its God, Brueggemann finds a story of God's people *with God's land.* "Biblical faith is a pursuit of historical belonging that includes a sense of destiny derived from such belonging." Belonging requires *a sense of place,* a home place where persons can be secure, where meaning and well-being can be enjoyed without pressure or coercion.

In Brueggemann's view the covenant between Yahweh and the children of Israel involves the gift of a place, the land of Israel. With the gift come responsibilities for the people of the promise, responsibilities which involve care of the land, justice in its distribution, and a sense of safeguarding the gift for the future generations who will also be people of the gift. Paramount in this covenant relationship is the sense that the land is not a personal or private possession; rather it belongs to the whole community of the covenant, including children and children's children.

2. Reflecting on the human condition, and no doubt informed by the experiences of the sixties, Brueggemann argues that a sense of place is both a primary human need and a fundamental category of faith. He draws a distinction between space and place. Space denotes "an arena of freedom, without coercion or accountability, free of pressures and void of authority." Place, however, "is a different matter":

Place is space which has historical meanings, where some things have happened which are now remembered and which provide continuity and identity across generations. Place is space in which important words have been spoken which have established identity, defined vocation, and envisioned destiny. Place is space in which vows have been exchanged, promises have been made, and demands have been issued.[20]

The distinction between space and place is crucial for the theme of this book. A sense of place requires that places be distinguishable from blank space. It depends upon the sort of words, vows, and historical meanings Brueggemann points to as the hallmarks of place, but also upon the intrinsic qualities of places themselves as we image them in art, poetry, and song.

Perhaps Brueggemann's definition is overly dependent upon history and human activity as the distinguishing characteristics of place. But the connection between place and our essential humanness is of great importance. Brueggemann is surely correct when he insists that "place is indeed a protest against the unpromising pursuit of space. It is a declaration that our humanness cannot be found in escape, detachment, absence of commitment, and undefined freedom."[21]

This sense of the importance of place in human life and community is borne out by the work of humanistic geographers, such as Anne Buttimer. Buttimer reports that a sense of personal identity is intimately bound up with "place identity," and that humans display marked patterns of "territoriality." So embedded are these qualities that we can live unconscious of their presence, until they are threatened. Once a place identity or territory is threatened, our behaviors speak volumes concerning the importance of these matters for our fundamental human functioning.[22] For example, Australia's unique landscape is presently being celebrated in film, poetry, and literature, just at the time when its ecological fragility and the delicate balance of its unique environment are being threatened. Our sense of place, reflected in art and literature, often coalesces only when that place is threatened. We must see the celebration of the Australian landscape as bound up with the widespread sense of environmental threat experienced by many perceptive Australians, such as Kath Walker and Judith Wright.

Expressed in poetry and song, in painting and in film, a sense of place is a central element of how one makes meaning in life. As such, it is an integral part of religious faith. In the transition to our mobile, urban life style, we have moved away from a sense of place. The community and commitment which places once signified seem to be casualties of our recent history. Indeed, as Cox and Brueggemann agree, we have sought the freedom of space at the expense of the places of roots, commitment, and community.

3. For Brueggemann human history cannot be read as a record of evolution, a progression toward an always richer and more humane future. Indeed, when we look at recent history, there is an element of uncertainty, of ambiguity, of randomness. Further, for Brueggemann history cannot be set over against space. If Cox saw the biblical faith as a nonspatial historical faith, Brueggemann sees it as a placed history. For Brueggemann a meaning grows out of historical experience in a place, so that a sense of place is a central element of how one makes meaning in life, a central element of faith. The hermeneutics of recent theologies, both the existentialist and the "mighty acts of God" schools, stressed event to the neglect of structure, history to the disregard of nature. This hermeneutical bias made it impossible for them to appreciate the land as a central theological motif.[23] The notion of placed history may be an important affirmation about the character of human life, of its sense of homelessness and its yearning for home.

Beyond their differences both Cox and Brueggemann have something to teach us about the method and styles of theology in times as diverse as the sixties and the eighties. In relation to both the secular city and the land their works point out some deep and seldom-raised issues about the role of place in human community and human faith. How do the places which we inhabit shape whom we become and how we think of our God? In turn, how does our control of the environment shape the ways in which we image ourselves and our faith? It is against the backdrop of these considerations that we will be able to respond with some measure of insight to the crises of the closing decade of the century.[24]

Cox's reading of secularization is important and has continuing relevance. While his unilinear, evolutionary view of history has taken some serious knocks in the transition to the eighties, it is clear that Cox has grasped an essential element of biblical faith.[25] In pointing to the historicity of Israel's faith, to the God of the Exodus as the God of history, Cox has brought elements of that faith to light, but at the risk of deemphasizing other elements of biblical faith.

In particular, we must note the way in which Cox has contrasted time and space, history and spatialization, always in favor of the former. It is ironic that, in a work taking its name from a place, the secular city, Cox has pointed us away from place toward time as the key to theological interpretation. In his discussion of space and place Brueggemann goes much of the way toward demonstrating the importance of place. However, he seems still to root the definition of place in the human activity which "hallows" or "qualifies" the otherwise empty space. I will argue that a sense of place is as much a function of the nature of the places themselves as it is of human activity. At this point both Cox and Brueggemann merely reflect what has been a largely unquestioned assumption of modern theology; namely, that history is the horizon of all that is, that creation is understood only in the context of history. This view exists in considerable tension with emphases within the Bible, and especially the Old Testament.

By counterposing the historicizing of God and the spatialization of God, Cox appears to have lost sight of the very important biblical link between God and the land. Here

Brueggemann adds a necessary corrective. If Yahweh is the God of history, there are some important senses in which Yahweh is also the God of nature. Further, in his enthusiasm for the city Cox has largely ignored the continuing importance of the town and the whole complex of rural life. What he does not see is that an ecological network binds rural areas to the cities, just as every life form in some way depends upon every other life form, and the whole survives only in balance and cooperation.

At this time in our history Brueggemann finds us rootless, on a path of loss and disintegration. The great promise which Cox associated with the city has failed to speak to our need for place or to address the category of faith which Brueggemann has uncovered. Offering us mobility and anonymity—and with these the escape from ties, freedom to experiment, and release from the kinds of commitment that found community—the secular city has not brought us closer to faith. Rather, it may have moved us further from it. In the terms of Brueggemann's analysis the secular city never offered "place"; it only offered "space." And space is an empty concept for us, geometrical and gridlike, neither poetic nor theological. The problem is, following Cox's direction, that the modern notion of space has become equivalent to profane space, for we have lost the sense of sacred space.

In passages marked by a kind of nostalgia for a sensibility lost to us moderns and postmoderns, Mircea Eliade writes movingly of the sense of sacred space that is fundamental to preindustrial religions. Sacred space is the arena for renewal and sustenance of members of religious society. It is "full of being" and contrasts to the chaos and nonbeing of profane space. Although writing of religious societies, Eliade offers some telling insight into the plight of nonreligious persons. For if we have lost the sense of sacred space, we have by no means lost the needs that such space addresses, the needs for a cosmos of meaning and a center of being. Describing the role of religious rituals in religious societies in such activities as settling a territory, building a dwelling, or coming to inhabit a new place, Eliade seems to touch on perennial needs of human persons. For none of these activities is outside the experience of modern industrial societies, and each is especially present in postcolonial societies such as our own. We have settled territories and built whole cities of dwellings, but have we come truly to inhabit these places? The European settlement of these continents still requires that we address the meaning of settlement and habitation at a religious and theological level. Can we truly inhabit these continents without a sense of their unique sacredness?

The absence of a sense of sacred space is surely linked with the loss of a sense of place. The issues of place identity and the space that is full of being are intimately linked. Indeed, the religious concept of sacred space always seems to involve a view of space that centers around place. Now I think Cox is correct in suggesting that it is not possible for us to resacralize space. But it may be possible for us to regain a sense of place. And the recovery of a sense of place may be the means whereby the functions of sacred space can be regained in our secular culture. The places that we know and love can become the type of space that will nourish our lives at their deepest levels. Further, by reviving a sense of place we may be able to reactivate the care of the environment, which grows out of a sense of the sanctity and worth of particular places.

4. TOWARD A THEOLOGY OF THE LAND

The context and the direction for our own work is now set. If the rural crisis and the attendant problems of environmental degradation and conflict over land rights set the context for a theology of the land, the recovery of the biblical importance of the land sets our immediate direction. In what follows we can draw hermeneutical clues from Brueggemann's distinction between space and place and his highlighting the importance of place in the Hebrew understanding of the land. The concept of place and the sense of place will be foundational in our discussion of

Aboriginal and Hebrew religion, in our survey of scientific and theological views of space, and finally in our interpretation of the Incarnation and the incarnational lifestyle.

It is important at this point to say a few words about "theology of the land" and to ask ourselves how this undertaking relates to such themes as a theology of nature or theology of creation. At the outset it must be stressed that a deliberate decision is involved in undertaking a theology of the land. It is a question of focus and of theological method. "Land" in biblical usage points to a concrete historical phenomenon with which is associated a definite theology. Our attention to this theology will follow the work of Brueggemann, W. D. Davies, and others. A focus upon the biblical concept of land will give us a concrete vision that can be brought to bear on contemporary dilemmas. Further, we must differentiate this work from theologies of the earth, of creation, and of nature.

"Earth" and "land" are both legitimate translations of the Hebrew *'eretz,* but each is used in different contexts with different connotations. "Earth" is especially used in the context of creation narratives, while "land" is at home in the historical narratives of Israel's struggle for national and religious identity. If "earth" points to the physical basis and environment for life, "land" points to territory that is possessed, struggled over, used, and perhaps exploited. Brueggemann suggests that earth offers "a paradigm of an untroubled place for life which is not historically located or socially differentiated." By contrast, land is "a concrete, historical phenomenon that participates in all the ambiguities of political and economic power and is never uncomplicated or uncontaminated."[26]

Theologies of the earth, picking up on the Genesis narratives, typically grow out of creation themes. Such theologies deal in the immediacy of our relation with the earth and develop a range of connotations of nurturing, motherhood, fertility, and so on. They may speak of the blessings of the return to "Mother Nature." Like theologies of creation, such theologies tend to view the earth as the

31

physical basis and environment for life. A danger that frequently emerges in such theologies is the tendency toward a certain romanticism. Here, it seems, the biblical usage is instructive. The Hebrew Scriptures are particularly unsentimental about the land, providing us a very realistic picture of the assets and the liabilities of land and its occupation. Certainly we must be open to the holistic overtones present in "earth talk," just as we must recognize the value in traditions of the earth which question some of our exploitative economic attitudes. But it seems to me that there is value to be gained from a closer following of biblical emphases. In particular, if we are to respect biblical realism and the urgency of our context, we should avoid any appearance of sentimentality.

The word "land" brings us deeply into the movement of biblical history. The word relates to the concrete redemptive activity of God on Israel's behalf. For this reason I prefer theology of the land over theology of creation. The latter, while certainly a legitimate direction of theological reflection, seems to skew debate away from the biblical focus upon God's redemptive activity. By stressing the original goodness of God's creation, creation theology often posits a too simple return to the garden of life. Contemporary experience should warn us that no simple return to Eden is available. Only redemption opens the way for us, and this path is costly and difficult. Creation theologies too often pass lightly over the hazards and jeopardies of the human experience. It seems truer to the biblical focus to let the theme of redemption be our starting point, and in that context to shape a theology of the land.

Finally, theology of the land is distinct from natural theology and theology of nature. A theology of the land is, first, a more modest undertaking, reflecting as it does on the biblical tradition of God's dealings with humanity in terms of the land. Second, a theology of the land seeks to hold firmly onto the concreteness of the biblical tradition. Talk about "nature" draws us into a wider range of philosophical considerations that may lead us away from the sharpness of the biblical testimony. To speak of nature is immediately to enter into old distinctions and dichotomies: nature and grace, the natural and the supernatural, the natural and the human-made. Already the land is turned into an instance of something else, and a generalizing vision begins to blur the outlines.

Very interesting and important work is being done in our time in natural theology by a range of scholars, including especially the work of the process theologians. The value of this work lies in its insistence that our concepts of the environment ultimately are rooted in our understanding of the underlying nature of reality itself. Yet this may seem to go too far in the direction of generality and to offer too little of direct relevance for our theological and environmental inquiries. Further, the relation of process theologies to what Paul Santmire calls "the deepest roots of Western religious sensibility and vocabulary" is largely undeveloped. Our concern is rather with those roots, seeking a faithful development of the theological implications of the biblical focus on the land. While these problems may need to be addressed theologically, it lies beyond the scope of this book to undertake that work.

This is not to suggest that we are to confine ourselves narrowly to repeating biblical categories, nor that the results of our inquiry may not have implications for a theology of nature. However, there seems to be wisdom in tackling one problem at a time, and then letting the broader issues emerge. For too long, theology has prided itself on giving the most general account and addressing the most general questions. The wisdom of that approach is being questioned these days, with the emergence of local theologies and the emphasis upon theologies of the people. We are learning again to think more modestly and to set limits on our own grandiosity. With this measure of modesty and ambition, then, we direct our attention to theology of the land.

As the people of Aboriginal and Christian religious faith faced the armed forces of the state of Western Australia, the question of the land came into sharp focus. Tradable resource or religious inheritance? Commodity or gift? In the dynamic struggle with heralds of the kingdom of God, land is never simply empty space awaiting human redemption. For some, like the Aborigines, it is intrinsically holy, while for others it bears the imprint of God. For Christian faith the land is always gift, bearing in many ways the stamp of the Creator upon it. It is interesting to note how soil conservationists like Dean Graetz fall into language which sees the land as itself active, having its own being, its own memory. Graetz remarks, "We've forgotten but the land never forgets." What is land? What is space? To answer these questions we will turn in the next chapter to a closer look at Brueggemann's book and to the lessons that may be learned from the Australian Aboriginal people.

CHAPTER TWO

The Centrality of Land in Aboriginal and Hebrew Religion

One of earth's most ancient peoples, the Australian Aborigines, answers the question "What is the land?" in these terms:

> The land is my mother. Like a human mother, the land gives us protection, enjoyment, and provides for our needs—economic, social and religious. We have a human relationship with the land: Mother–daughter, son. When the land is taken away from us or destroyed, we feel hurt because we belong to the land and we are part of it.
>
> To survive, [we] have to know about the land. The land contains our information about our traditional way of life. It's written there. It's like a library for our people and children. So we must preserve it. It's very sad when mining wipes out our library and there's nothing left for our children to get their education from. . . .
>
> Land is a breathing place for my people.[1]

At a time when the problems we face in the environment are global in their dimensions, a time when as a human species our fate is increasingly a common fate, it is most important that we open ourselves to voices from within the human community which we do not normally hear. The Australian Aboriginal people have something vital to say to

35

the Christian community throughout the world. It is time, I believe, for us to listen to and learn from people who were Australians before Captain James Cooke and Governor Arthur Phillip. These were persons who cared for the lands out of some deeply held religious convictions. European possession of these lands was a dispossession of another race of people who had lived in them for millennia. And in those millennia the land retained its fertility and its beauty. Perhaps not all Aboriginal practices were ecologically sound—and certainly populations were comparatively small and technologies simple—but theirs was a living in harmony with the natural capacities of the environment. Over the long period of their inhabitation they adapted successfully to the environment.

By contrast, our brief habitations have drawn untold wealth out of this environment and raised unimagined volumes of food and grain. Yet these results have been purchased at great cost to the environment. Our rates of soil degradation, cited in chapter 1, become monstrous when compared with a negligible rate of soil degradation caused by our predecessors. In comparison with them, how little have we cared for the land, how little have we come to understand this place, how little have we come to love it as a homeland. We have much to learn about what it means to "possess" a place, to "occupy" a land. Much of this we can learn from indigenous peoples like the Australian Aborigines and the American Indians.

We should acknowledge at the outset that there are many difficulties in our way. Anthropologist W. E. Stanner says, "It requires a considerable effort of mind and imagination for a European to come to grips with [Australian Aboriginal religion]."[2] Perhaps the greatest hindrance to European comprehension of tribal people's thought and life comes from twin attitudes of cultural superiority and romanticizing the culture and life style of the tribal people.

As we desire deeper unity and coherence in our own fragmented lives, we may be tempted to look at traditional cultures such as the Aboriginal with rose-colored spectacles.

It is possible then to project our own lost innocence onto the Aboriginal people and be blinded to the realities of their struggle for existence, a struggle no less precarious than our own. By romanticizing Aboriginal culture we again avoid the really difficult task of contact and comprehension. Fortunately the sciences of ethnology and anthropology have advanced to the point that we are able to lay many of the misconceptions to rest. Much of our arrogance is based on untenable evolutionary concepts of human progress.

When the vast work of clearing away these false assumptions has been completed, we may be in a position to appreciate the wealth of Aboriginal cultural achievement and to begin to understand the viability and relevance of their adaptation to this land. The same can be said for the understanding of the North American Indian. Arrogance and romanticism have for too long colored the relations between the European and the indigenous peoples of North America. Progress in one area can spark progress in another. It may well be that at the level of our mutual dependence upon these threatened landscapes and the thin layer of topsoil which is our only long-term hope for survival, European settlers and indigenous peoples may find their first real meeting ground.

To do this we must first orient ourselves to cultural patterns alien to our own. In such cultures the role of religion is more pervasive than in our own, and the relation to the natural environment is a central factor in both religion and culture. Land and the human relationship to land are central to the whole way of life and are deeply embedded in the fabric of religious practice, thought, and ritual. Further, the issues of land are integrated into religion by means of the concept of "sacred space." In simple terms this means that religious societies see a fundamental division in space between the sacred and the profane. Mircea Eliade maintains that such societies have a specifically nonhomogeneous view of space, which contrasts with our scientific homogeneous view of space.[3]

Eliade expresses the distinction in ontological terms, that

is, in terms of being and nonbeing, of existence and destruction. Sacred space is that which is "full of being" and thus strengthens and enhances the being of human persons. Profane space is the space of chaos and nonbeing, which threatens the life of human persons with destruction and death. In religious societies there is no distinction between the physical and the psychic, between the social and the spiritual needs of persons. The word "being" expresses that totality. If sacred space is full of being, it is full of all that makes for life—food, shelter, emotional and psychic support, spiritual nurture. Further, life depends equally upon the provision of food and the nurture of the psyche or spirit. Beyond this lies the notion of a continuum in which human life is not separate from that of the land, the plants, and the animals, nor from the spirits of ancestors and other spirit beings.

Eliade's phenomenological analysis of religion and its relation to the land is a useful place to begin our attempt to relate the religious life of indigenous societies with that of our own. Eliade distinguishes between religious and nonreligious societies. In religious societies religion forms the basis for social structure and human life. In nonreligious societies, such as our own, religion is one factor among others, serving specific functions in the lives of some individuals but not forming the substratum upon which the whole society is founded. Such societies, sometimes called advanced or industrial, are marked by a pluralism of religious beliefs and a range within each belief system from true believers to nonbelievers.

In religious societies questions of belief and nonbelief do not arise in the way they do in ours. These are profound differences. They make it difficult for persons of nonreligious cultures, even religious people who live in a nonreligious culture, to comprehend the thought and life orientations of persons of religious cultures. This is certainly one of the fundamental problems in the relationships between European Australians and Australians of Aboriginal descent. In relation to the issue of land and land rights the disjunction between understandings is almost total. With this general account in mind, let us turn to consider the religion and the relationship to the land of the Australian Aboriginal people.

1. LAND IN ABORIGINAL RELIGION

The foundation of all the Aboriginal cultures is the "Dreamtime," or better "the Dreaming." The Dreaming refers to a primeval time which continues into the present, a time in which the processes of shaping the world into its present form took place, making it habitable for human populations. The concept is fluid, bringing together many elements of religion which we tend to separate. Not only a creation myth, the Dreaming speaks of the power of geographical sites and their role in determining issues of personal nature and vocation of those born on or near them.

In the Dreaming occurs a vast series of events that transform the empty, featureless plains of the earth into their present form. Before the Dreaming the earth existed as it had always existed, as a large flat disk, floating in space. Earth was in fact an area of homogeneous space.

> Its uninhabited surface was a vast featureless plain, extending unbroken to the horizon. No hills or watercourses broke its monotonous surface, no trees or grass covered its nakedness, nor did the calls of birds or animals disturb its quiet. It was a dead world. Yet slumbering beneath that monotonous surface were indeterminate forms of life that would eventually transform it into the world which the Aborigines know today.[4]

Across this wide earth the ancestor heroes wandered, and in the places they rested they brought features into existence, hills and valleys, rock pools, trees and vegetation. In some cases the ancestors metamorphosed themselves into such features and landmarks. The tracks of these primeval wanderings are still known and revered by Aboriginal peoples, whose pilgrimages, or walkabouts, follow the ancient trails and link up ancient sacred sites. These are journeys in which the traveling itself is important, for it reestablishes the "pilgrims" in their living relation to the Dreaming.

In seeking to grasp the set of interrelated meanings that make up the Dreaming, Australian philosopher Max Charlesworth lists four elements:

—"a narrative mythical account of foundation and shaping of the entire world by ancestor heroes who are uncreated and eternal";

—"the embodiment of the spiritual powers of the ancestor heroes in the land, in certain sites, in species of flora and fauna, so that this power is available to people today";

—"a general way of life or 'law' ";

—"the personal 'way' or vocation that an individual Aboriginal might have by virtue of his membership of a clan, or by virtue of his spirit-conception relating him to particular sites."

The intimate relationship between human society and the land is established in the Dreaming. As Charlesworth writes, "For the Aboriginal his land is a kind of religious icon, since it represents the power of the Dreamtime beings and also effects and transmits that power." Although these beings are credited with creative powers, they are not separable from the land itself, and are "intrinsically part of the land."[5]

The truly fascinating element of this conception is its dynamic character, the way in which it transforms empty space into places—recognized and known, beloved, remembered, celebrated. Places too are transformed into a subtle and complex web. If the pre-Dreaming world is homogeneous and featureless, then the Dreaming establishes tracks upon the trackless, places within the vast emptiness of space. Land is seen as an integral part of the web of life, physical and spiritual, not inert, empty, passive. In Eliade's term, all the land is, in a sense, sacred. For the tribes who occupy it, it is fully of being, the very source of their life and sustenance. This dynamic, living understanding of the land has sophisticated ecological and social implications.

In the Aboriginal view the forms of the land may not be tampered with carelessly. There is here a respect for the given forms of the land, and beyond that for the patterns of animal and plant life that have evolved over the millennia. Thus A. E. Newsome reports how the mythology of the red kangaroo among the Aranda people is developed in a way that stabilizes the life of the kangaroo.[6] Further, the navigational utility of the Aboriginal mythology and its value in orientation and direction has been verified by numerous experiences. The navigational expert David Lewis traveled in sections of the western desert over a total of 7,800 kilometers with a small group of Aboriginal men of the region. He writes:

> All my preconceived ideas about "land navigation" turned out to be wrong. In place of the stars, sun, winds and waves that guide Pacific Island canoemen, the main references of the Aborigines proved to be the meandering tracks of the ancestral Dreaming beings that form a network over the whole Western Desert. . . .
>
> When an Aboriginal depicts a stretch of country he generally incorporates its mythical with its physical features, so stressing the inseparable interrelation between the two. Such paintings cannot be interpreted without inside knowledge, yet their emphasis on the spiritual attributes of places makes them doubly memorable to the initiated. . . . This investing of particular places with emotionally charged significance must have been an important survival factor for hunter–gatherers living in such a harsh environment. . . . For the Aboriginal the world is filled with things which have meaning. All with whom I travelled demonstrated extraordinary acuity of perception of natural signs and ability to

interpret them, and almost total recall of every topographical feature. A single visit forty years ago would have been sufficient to make an indelible imprint.[7]

In these examples we see that for the Aborigine the vast ranges of space are turned into identifiable places. Places are identified by means of the Dreaming wanderings in such a way that traditional Aborigines develop an amazing acuity for discerning and remembering sites. Given the vast, trackless nature of the Australian interior, this capacity had very obvious survival value and a wide range of pragmatic uses. The contrast to the European attitude and resultant capacity to remember and identify places is almost total. A white Australian crossing the Nullabor Plain in a bus said to me: "Look, there's nothing there." We saw nothing because of our prior understanding of what counted as "something." In general, Europeans find these spaces empty and forbidding. But for the Aborigines they are alive and teeming with life-giving energies.

The Aboriginal understanding of land regulates distribution of land and its bounty. Land distribution is achieved on a fairly equitable and humane basis by means of the "ownership" of parts of the myth cycle by different groups. Aboriginal myths are extremely local, relating to particular sites, fixing borders, detailing "limits beyond which a myth could not be told, nor song sung, nor ceremonies performed." The possession of myth cycles relating to the Dreaming establishes the relationship of tribes and the smaller local descent groups to a range of territories. In retelling the stories and enacting the related rituals the possessors of the mythology reaffirm their relationship to this land and reactivate the powers and sanctions of the Dreaming. Amos Rapoport notes, "Tribal borders are respected. Even friendly tribes do not have the right to enter each other's land at will; outsiders may enter an area un-invited only in an emergency (e.g., when starving) and have to recompense the owners."[8] Sharing of one's food with another who is starving is not a matter of charity for the

Aborigines. Such hospitality is a duty, which expresses the fact that in a harsh ecosystem each part is dependent upon every other part.

Further relationships are established by the place or circumstances of conception or birth. Being conceived or born at a particular place sets up a totemic relationship whereby an individual is related to the particular creature associated with the site—ant, lizard, kangaroo, etc. Thus an individual attains membership in a totemic group which in its own way defines a set of relationships to other creatures and to sacred sites. Individuals are bound to specific sites and animal or plant species, establishing a "web of life." In this way human persons are themselves parts of nature, "not opposed to other parts of it but bound to them by strong emotional ties, a kind of empathy."[9] Within the territory of a tribe each group has a ritual and social locus and an area whose main importance is economic. Together these form what Rapoport calls the "ecological life space."

Clearly the Aboriginal view does not separate the economic from the spiritual. The human person is related to the whole complex of life—the land in its natural conditions, its spiritual origins and continuing significance, and the life of the plants and animals—by the dynamic concept of the Dreaming. Each myth cycle, with its accompanying rituals, is concerned with "maintaining a life that is considered to have commenced at the beginning of time; brings vital life-giving power to bear on the affairs of men."[10] Expressed in art and designs executed on sacred objects—pieces of flat board known as *churinga*—the Dreaming surrounds the Aboriginal in every aspect of daily life.

Berndt sums up the significance of Aboriginal mythology in terms of a set of relationships which bind human life to nature: "Man is seen as being part of nature, and in harmony with it. Without that recognized harmony, semi-nomadic existence would have been very difficult indeed: it under-lines that need for patience and an assurance that renewal is a basic factor of living."[11] There is a continuum of life from the ancestral heroes of the Dreaming to human persons, through the living animals and plants, down to the land itself. Humans exist then in a threefold set of relationships: between human beings themselves, with a strong emphasis on cooperation, division of labor, and participation; between human beings and the mythic characters, which creates commitment to actions consistent with the spiritual conception of the land; and between Aboriginal persons and the natural environment. This network of relationships forms a point of connection with early Hebrew religion, in which the notion of covenant established a similarly inclusive set of relationships.

There is a remarkable parallel to our own experience in the Aboriginal view of space and place. The vast, featureless plain of the pre-Dreaming world bears striking resemblance to the homogeneous space of our scientific world view. Even more frighteningly, it calls to mind the denuded spaces of our rural landscape, or the final scenario of nuclear holocaust. Could it be that what Aboriginal mythology looks *back* to, we must look *forward* to as the end of our cultural trajectory? In some visionary way we may perhaps find in this mythology a sobering foretelling of our future. It is important, however, to set side by side with this vision the transforming nature of the Dreaming. Just as the Dreaming transformed that empty homogeneity of space into the variety of lived places, could a New Dreaming transform our space in places, habitable by human communities, sustaining and full of being? Do we have in our religious tradition such a Dreaming?

Many of these questions must await a later chapter for their fuller treatment. But in turning now to some of the Scriptures underlying Christianity, we begin to explore the "Dreaming" of the Christian faith. This brief exposure to Aboriginal religion will help to highlight an aspect of Hebrew faith that has often been obscured: the importance of the land in that faith. The first way in which the Aboriginal people have something vital to say to Christians relates to the rediscovery of the centrality of the land in the early Hebrew Scriptures.

2. LAND IN THE EARLY HEBREW SCRIPTURES

In the early Hebrew Scriptures we find a series of parallels between the religion of this people in its relation to the land and the religion of the Aboriginal people. We shall consider the centrality of the land in both these religious societies, the network of relationships which bind the people to one another and to the land they occupy, and the endurance of notions of spiritual inheritance and spiritual possession through periods of dispossession and exile.

The Centrality of the Land

Recent study of the Hebrew Scriptures has accentuated the importance of the land for the faith of the Hebrews. The suggestion has been made that land in the early Hebrew Scriptures does not simply provide the setting for the emergence of the Hebrew faith, but actually partakes of the substance of the faith. Brueggemann's claim that "land is a central, if not *the central theme* of biblical faith" is striking in its boldness.[12] Indeed, Brueggemann suggests the reigning "orthodoxies" of the last several decades in Old Testament studies have tended to obscure the fact that Hebrew faith in Yahweh cannot be understood apart from the gift of the land. Beginning with the centrality of this gift, Brueggemann perceives the entire sweep of biblical history in terms of three land-related movements, each of which draw its basic definition from the land.

The first is the history *to the land*. Forged in times of dispossession, in Egypt and the wilderness, the Hebrew faith looked forward to the time when God would give the people a land of their own. The voluntary and forced migrations which form the prehistory of this people were migrations in search of the land of promise.

The second is the history *in the land*. Life in the land turned out to be not at all the comfortable affair some had expected. God's people learned that their safety and prosperity in the land depended upon their faithfulness to the law of God and specifically to the stipulations of God's covenant, by which the land was deeded to them. In the period of the kings the role of the prophet was accentuated; in these times the temptations of greedy accumulation of property and proud assertion of personal invincibility were often too much for the people or the kings to resist. Time and again God sent prophets to kings and subjects to remind them of the covenant and of their responsibilities to God under this covenant.

The third is the history *from exile to land*. A time of dispossession became one of the very creative moments in Jewish history. New understandings were drawn from old texts, and a new language, that of apocalyptic, emerged to speak of new experiences and new hopes. But it is still hope for the land, the expectation of original restoration, that serves as the guiding principle of this period.

In all this history the issue of land is central. The struggles of faith, the struggles to be a people and to live with kings and foreign powers, are all concentrated in the issue of the land, how the land is to be properly possessed, how the land is to figure in covenant fidelity. Just as land is a central element in the religion of the Australian Aborigine, so there is a similar centrality in the religion of the ancient Hebrews. One cannot think of the land apart from the rule of God, and that rule issues in quite specific requirements in the form of the covenant.

Covenant Relationships

A pattern of relationships, similar to that which bound the Aborigines to their land, is operative in the covenant relationship established by God with the ancient Hebrews. There are several aspects of this which must be stressed. First, the land is God's, and so it did not belong to the Hebrews. Their inheritance and occupation of the land was wholly dependent upon the grace of God who gave it to them. True, the land was to be their "inheritance for ever," but that must not be taken to mean that they would always dwell in the land. Given by God, it was not theirs by an individual or personal right; it was theirs by a deeper divine right, and that implied both a set of conditions and an ultimately unbreakable inheritance.

A common implication of both the Aboriginal and the Hebrew sense of land possession can now be indicated. For the Aborigine the notion of possession, as such, simply does not make sense. He sees it the other way: the land possesses him. The land does not belong to the Aborigines; the Aborigines belong to the land, and only in this sense is it "theirs." For this reason two centuries of white dispossession has in no way altered the Aboriginal sense of belonging to the land. Similarly, in the history of the Hebrews, foreign powers—Assyria, Babylon, Persia—might come and take possession. But the land was no more theirs than Australia belongs to the whites. The covenant of God with the Hebrews whereby God gave them the land was not abrogated by the might of nations or the passage of history. They, like the Aborigines, knew something of the true nature of possession that was, and is still, hidden from their conquerors.[13]

A second point to consider is that the behavior of the people of the land was governed by God's law. In the Aboriginal case the Dreaming itself also means law, the way of right living. In Hebrew faith only faithfulness to the covenant regulations could ensure the well-being of the people in the land. For both peoples, then, possession of land entailed moral obligation. Only as one was conscious and deliberate about the moral obligation that goes with possession could there be any sense of peace or harmony in dwelling in the land. For the Hebrew people this matter related centrally to the relationship of the nation to its God.

Third, the gift of the land was to the whole community and was to be distributed justly. Land must be divided between groups and individuals, but the gift was to the entire nation. Distribution to the various tribes had to be equitable. Further, the provision of the year of jubilee subjected all possession of land to reassignment every fifty years. While there is no evidence that the jubilee was ever practiced in relation to land redistribution, its presence in Scripture stands as a powerful sign of the will of the Lord. No one could treat the land as if it were his own private possession, but all had to consider the needs of the neighbor, including the stranger who dwelt in their midst. Equity and justice flow from the Hebrew understanding of the gift of God to the whole community. The rights of the yet unborn must also be considered in relation to their inheritance of this land. Land that is given to a community must be preserved and maintained so that gift may be passed on intact.

Finally, the land itself is part of a covenantal set of relationships. Although, in Eliade's terms, land may be sacred space for both the Aborigines and the Hebrews, the precise ways in which that applied differ. For the Aborigines the distance between themselves, the places they inhabit, and the Dreaming ancestors is not great. Theirs is a faith of participation and interpenetration. Consequently their relation to the land is one built upon sympathetic harmony. All partake of the all. For the Hebrews the sense of God as creator, and humanity as the image of God, played a significant role in separating God from the land and humans from the land.

The Hebrews did not see themselves as partaking in a mystical oneness with the land and its creatures. They saw themselves as separate. But that separation cannot be used to argue that they became indifferent to other creatures or that they arrogated to themselves the right to rule over nature, as some have suggested. Indeed, an important implication of the covenantal view of land occupation is that all behavior, including behavior relating to the land itself and its various creatures, is covered by God's law. We find in the early works of the Torah a catalog of rules and regulations which specify in great detail what behaviors are unacceptable to the Giver of the land.

It is in this context that the important theme of dominion must be considered. Genesis 1:26 reads: "Then God said, 'Let us make man in our image, after our likeness; and let them have dominion over the fish of the sea, and over the birds of the air, and over the cattle, and over all the earth,

and over every creeping thing that creeps upon the earth.' "
The granting to humanity of "dominion" over all the other
creatures has become something of a cause célèbre among
ecologists of various schools. It has been seen as the
foundation of a dangerously human-centered view of the
cosmos and as the basis of a willful human arrogance in
relation to the variety of God's creatures. For some, all talk
of dominion is a product of "hierarchical" thinking that
poisons human relationships and undermines proper respect
for the integrity of creation.

Yet understood in the context of Hebrew faith many of
these objections cannot be sustained. The creation accounts of
Genesis must be set in the framework of the covenant with
God, which is foundational for the entire Hebrew Scriptures.
In this covenant no gift is without its obligations and
responsibilities. Thus the gift of dominion carried with it
profoundly demanding expectations. The passage itself
suggests something of the depth of these obligations by linking
the gift of dominion with the image of God. As creatures in the
image of God, human persons must exercise a dominion
fashioned on that of God. The image of God carries the
highest imaginable set of expectations; namely, that one will
live in relation to all God's creatures with the love and care
that God exercises. Arrogance or willfulness are as inappro-
priate here as would be a cessation of God's care for God's
creatures. Indeed, if we suggest that "dominion" is really
another way of saying "responsibility," then the gift of
dominion is foundational to ecological consciousness.[14]

The charge of human-centeredness can only be sustained if
one abstracts the place of humanity from the whole order of
creation. To be in the image of God is not to arrogate to
humanity a place of independence from the rest of creation.
Rather it is to assign humans a determinate place in the order
of being, as lower than God but higher than other creatures.
This place carries a heavy burden of responsibility, both to
God above and to creation beneath.[15] In the modern loss of
the sense not only of God but also of the order of creation, the
image of God has been misconstrued and seen to arrogate to

humanity the characteristics of an independent god. But such a view is an abstraction, endorsed by neither the words of Genesis nor the teaching of the entire canon of Scripture.

Undoubtedly human arrogance and indifference lie at the heart of our dismal record of environmental destruction. But these cannot be traced to the Hebrew notion of dominion as it emerges from a careful study of the whole canon of Scripture. Indeed, the multiple laws relating to the care of animals and land in the Hebrew Scriptures tell of quite a different attitude. So detailed are these laws that it makes little sense to see them as solely a concern for property. These concerns carry over into the teaching of Jesus. As Robin Attfield remarks:

> The New Testament bespeaks God's care for animals such as sparrows (Matthew 10:29, Luke 12:6) and plants such as lilies (Matthew 7:28-30), just as much as the Old. There is no more reason to regard Jesus' advocacy of rescuing asses and oxen which have fallen into pits on the sabbath (Luke 14:5) as motivated solely by concern for property than the Old Testament provisions relating to the well-being of domestic animals.[16]

In the covenantal view of land tenure we see a set of relationships which define the nature of the possession. The relationships exhibit a threefold pattern similar to that noted in Aboriginal religion. There is, first, the relationship between human persons and their God; second, the relationships between the various members of the community, including the unborn children who will follow these present members; and third, the relation of the human persons to the land itself. Each of these relationships is regulated by the covenant understanding and its radical sense of the sovereignty of the God who gives the land to the faithful people.

This Hebrew understanding can richly inform a Christian theology of the land. The land, as God's creation and gift, is valued for its own sake. It has meaning and value far beyond its mere economic value. It is not a blank space upon which we write our history of dominance; rather, it is religious space upon which is written the story of God's dealing with us and our dealing with God. These dealings provide the enduring marks of our history on the land. Land is not held for purely personal gain; it is held in trust. This means that the inherent qualities, the limitations, and the capabilities of the land must be respected. As property held in trust it must be passed on intact to those members of the community who will follow us in possession.

Surviving the Exile

If various tribal peoples today live as exiles in their own country, they may find cause for sober reflection and even for hope in considering the third history of Israel, that of the exile. In this period the land covenant underwent radical upheaval. Here the children of Israel experienced drastic discontinuity in their relation to the land. Yet although history as they had known it seemed to be coming to an end, this period is one of tremendous creativity for Israel's faith. It is, I believe, especially relevant for the times in which we live, as we too experience change and discontinuity, the wrenching need to fashion a new sense of who we are as a people in relation to our environment.

In the experiences of the exiles Israel was ranged on the losing side of world history. Yet Israel managed to keep its faith. A small minority, deported from their own land and forcibly settled in an alien land, still retained a sense of national and spiritual identity. How was this possible? The answer lies largely in the contribution of the prophets. In the schools of such prophets as Jeremiah, Ezekiel, the Priestly Writer, and Second Isaiah there flourished a kind of thought and a kind of preaching that were to keep alive the traditions of the vanquished Israel.

These prophets were not afraid to think the thoughts that others preferred to pass over, nor to preach the words that others wished not to hear. In particular they were not afraid to name the judgment of God upon God's people. They did not confuse God's judgment with God's love, and thus could

51

see beyond and through God's judgment to God's love. Although this language was rooted in the covenantal faith, in the final analysis the prophets devised a new language and a new literature to bring the new history of God with God's people to expression.

Jeremiah taught that God would restore the fortunes of Israel and establish a new covenant (Jer. 30:18-22; 31:31-34). Faced with this word Israel had the choice between the data of present experience and the word of promise, as yet unsupported by any data. Some chose the word of promise, recognizing in it the only language that stood between themselves and rootlessness. Beyond the facts there was the language. Brueggemann draws a parallel to the experience of the German people after the Second World War. They too discovered, in the words of Heinrich Boll, that "this destroyed city is the homeland," and that the language of promise is the only way to be there.[17]

Ezekiel taught that Yahweh himself departs from the land and from the city, that Yahweh goes with the people into exile. If the people of Israel are exiled because they do not fulfill God's covenant, then God is exiled because of Israel's betrayal. Yet this suffering God is not finally defeated. In the exile the word of God comes again, telling of a new beginning of history, a new covenant history grounded in God's grace. In speaking of this new covenant the land is once again central (see Ezek. 37:1-14; 47:13ff; 48:29). Such is the reign of grace and covenant in this history that Israel must learn to share the distribution of the land with the stranger as with the native born.

It is in this context that the work of the *Priestly Writer* is to be read. The creation account of Genesis 1:1–2:4*a* is settled at this time, so that the accounts of creation out of chaos and the formless void do not have a merely prehistorical significance. At some level they must be seen as comments on the exilic experience of Israel. "It is in the context of exile that Israel told its best stories. . . . It is important that the exile is the time when all the old stories were placed into a fixed form."[18]

This reworking of old traditions is seen in *Second Isaiah*.

Thus the old land tradition of Abraham and Sarah is used in two places, 51:2-3 and 54:1-3. The experiences of Noah (54:9-10) and David (55:3) are brought to consciousness. This is a way of stressing the landed experiences of preexilic Israel, of asserting that the notions of inheritance and heritage are still the possession of the exiled nation. The language is still valid and active, even if the data of present history do not indicate their immediate fulfillment.

In all this work we see the spiritual genius of the Hebrew people. The stress upon the landed experience of preexilic Israel is a way of proclaiming that the notion of the eternal inheritance still has power and effect. All these traditions, of covenant and creation, speak of the free gift of land to Yahweh's covenant partner, Israel and this is now understood eschatologically. The language is kept alive, even as it is transformed into a new language of hope and promise for the future. In the new language of apocalyptic land is again seen as gift, the arena for divine holy intervention and transformation. Standing over against the experiences of land loss, of dispossession, this language asserts the reality of God's rule and the closeness of God's intervention to restore God's own people to their heritage.

3. LAND AND CHRISTIANITY

Christians have very often lost sight of the Hebrew foundations of their faith, and whenever they have done this their understanding of their own Christianity has been impoverished. For the fact is that Jesus was a Jew, and the life of the early Jesus community was grounded in Jewish faith. As a first-century Jew, Jesus' life was rooted in the land, its physical presence and its religious significance. As W. D. Davies aptly reminds us, Jesus belonged not only to time, but to space. "The need to remember the Jesus of History entailed the need to remember the Jesus of a particular land; and the space and spaces which he occupied took on significance."[19] Unless we grasp these facts and understand the entire New Testament in the context of the

Old, unless we set the historical Jesus firmly in the geographical locus of the land, we go far astray in our understanding of our Christian faith.

If our encounter with the land religion of the Australian Aborigines brings us back to consider the centrality of the land for the early Hebrew faith, it will enable us to be more insightful Christians. But there is a second way in which an encounter with Aboriginal religion can enable Christians to learn. The Aborigines can teach us that empty space can be transformed into meaningful place. If the Dreaming draws us back to the constitution of the world before human activity, it may also point us forward to the reconstitution of the world our activity has despoiled. The world that we know is being turned into a wasteland, a garbage dump. We have the image of a past Edenic paradise; yet however much we long to return to Eden, its gates are barred. What we need, instead, is a way to look forward. Is there such a way? Only if an event occurred that had power similar to that of the Dreaming. Only an event that could turn the empty, featureless plains of our world into the place of trees and rivers and hills. Only if our postindustrial landscapes of blight could once again be constituted as places for people, neighborhoods where life is sustained in spiritual and physical ways, where local options could once again be exercised in all the richness that inheres in just, humane community. Is there an event to which we could point? Is there an event that will reconstitute place for us?

It will be the argument of the rest of this book that such an event has occurred at the very center of Christian history. It is the event of no less than the Incarnation of God. That Incarnation grows out of the tradition of the Hebrew Scriptures, indeed, is of a piece with them. For if the land is the central theme of those Scriptures, the Incarnation becomes the central theme of the Christian Scriptures. More specifically, the engagement of the God of the Hebrews with the space and time of their history in the land comes to a fitting climax in the entry of that God into space and time in the person of Jesus Christ. To the tracing of these connections we now turn.

CHAPTER THREE

Shattering the Territorial Chrysalis: From the Exile to the Christian Scriptures

The religious importance of the land for two societies, far apart in history and widely separated by geography, stands before us. From both societies we may draw insight for our project. If the Australian Aboriginal society demonstrates to us the importance of a sense of place in human societies, the Hebrew society demonstrates the centrality of the land to the emerging Hebrew faith. While each of these societies stands far from us in both time and space, the Hebrew faith stands in intimate, organic relationship to the Christian faith. What is remarkable in the light of these insights is that from its very beginnings Christian thought moves *away* from any development of the issues of land or of place. Why is that? And what is its theological significance? A Christian theology of the land must face these serious questions.

Why is it, given the fundamental importance of place in human culture, given the central significance of the land in Hebrew religion, that Christian theology has developed scant tradition of theology of the land? There is no simple answer to this question, but a failure to grapple with it could lead to a fatal superficiality in our attempt to construct a Christian theology of the land. As Paul Santmire's work reminds us, any attempt to develop a theology of the land in the Christian tradition must engage that tradition at its deepest levels. Further, it must honestly face the ambiguity of Christianity's ecological promise.[1]

To engage this issue we must investigate two broad dimensions: the shaping of the biblical tradition and the development of the Western philosophical tradition. We are immediately confronted with some disturbing facts. First, there is practically no mention of the land in the New Testament. Second, the Western philosophical tradition has tended to move issues of place to the very periphery of philosophical reflection. In fundamental ways, then, our tradition predisposes us away from the issues of land and place. These two dimensions will occupy the next two chapters. In the present chapter we focus on the development and the interpretation of the biblical tradition with respect to land in the period following the exile. In the following chapter we turn to the development of the Western philosophical tradition.

In examining the development of the biblical tradition we immediately discover that references to the land become increasingly uncommon as we move into the later works of the Old Testament. In such biblical books as Job, Proverbs, Ecclesiastes, Song of Solomon, Esther, Jonah, and Daniel—that is, works of the exilic and postexilic periods—the issue of the land recedes in importance. When we turn to the New Testament Scriptures, we find that the issue has practically disappeared. Neither the words nor the concepts of land or of place play any significant role in the earliest literature of the Christian movement.

Two broad questions must now shape our inquiry. First, how are we to account for this apparent loss of a central motif of the early books of the Old Testament? Second, what is the theological significance of this development? Thus we are called upon to inquire both historically and theologically into the growth of the biblical tradition, especially as that tradition moves into the Christian Scriptures. I propose that there are three broad answers to these questions: the changing circumstances of the biblical peoples; the emergence of the new thought and language of apocalyptic; and the crisis provoked in the tradition by the event of Jesus Christ.

1. CHANGING CIRCUMSTANCES

The situation of the people of Israel changed dramatically with the exiles that began in the eighth century B.C.E. and culminated with the destruction of Jerusalem in the early sixth century. Overcome in the north by the Assyrians and later in the south by the Babylonians, the Hebrews were no longer a nation but a scattered people. No longer occupying one land, they were scattered to various parts of first the Persian and then the Greek empire. The importance of this diaspora for our theme is twofold.

First, the scattering of the people meant that their spiritual ties with the land and with the particular places in their country were placed under special stress. With the cessation of Israel as an independent state, focus moved from the territory of the former nation to the temple as the center of national life. On the one hand we see an intensification of the focus on place. Instead of the gift of the entire land, the sense of national identity is now focused in the temple. Davies puts it this way:

> After the Exile, the sentiment concerning The Land became concentrated in Jerusalem and the Temple, references to which in the sources used are very numerous. The absence of direct references to The Land can, therefore, be misleading, because The Land is implied in the city and the Temple which became its quintessence.[2]

This movement of focus should not be seen as a complete removal of the theme of the land, rather as its refinement and intensification.

But on the other hand, the physical and spiritual realities of living in another place were borne in upon the people. They discovered, with some difficulty to be sure, that God could be known in places other than the "promised land." This could not have other than a relativizing effect upon the notion that God's presence was to be limited to particular places. God could be worshiped in other places. Evidence suggests that in the early days of the Assyrian invasion a new sanctuary was founded at Shechem. Consecrated to the God of both Jerusalem and Shechem, it stood on the site of a former event in the life of the people, recorded in Deuteronomy 11:29.[3] Similarly, the Jews in Elephantine in Egypt established a temple and clearly proclaimed the possibility of the worship of Yahweh outside of Jerusalem.[4]

With the later return of some of the Jews to Jerusalem under the rule of the Persians, the cultic life of the nation was reconstituted in Jerusalem. But this renewal of the national cult had to coexist with the development of the cult outside of Jerusalem. It was, after all, a minority of the people who chose to return. The restoration of Jerusalem under Nehemiah, then, did not bring to an end the diaspora of the Jews nor to the diversification of holy places.

We see here two rather contrary movements, both of which were contained in the diverse experience of the diaspora. On the one hand, the sense of holy place is intensified in the focus upon the temple in Jerusalem. On the other hand, the experience of living in other places forced the realization that God cannot be tied down to one particular site, but may be worshiped in the places where God's people find themselves. Each of these movements, in its own way, moved attention away from the land as a whole as the national inheritance from Yahweh.

A second element of the changing circumstances of the Jewish people is the move from rural to urban locations. Increasingly the Jews became an urban people, affected by the Hellenistic culture that moved out through the trade routes of the ancient world. Whether our attention is on the Jews who returned in the fifth century to their own city or the Jews living throughout the cities of the ancient world, their social reality is increasingly an urban reality. As a result, their thought about the land tended to be in symbolic and anticipatory terms, rather than in the terms fostered by the pressures of daily land management.

With the sophistication of city life came the sophistication of Hellenistic thought. In its own way Hellenism was hostile to the landed traditions of the Hebrew faith and looked with scorn on many of the Hebrew understandings of the virtues of a life on the land. For Hellenistic thought the notion of locality was already dissolving in the emerging sense of a vast international empire, and in the speculations of Greek philosophers about the sweep of the celestial space. The movement of thought whereby place is swallowed up by space, which we shall trace in the next chapter, has its beginning here. Similarly, the early Christians were located in urban contexts. For them too the practical issues of the land tended to be irrelevant, except insofar as they shared in the apocalyptic expectation for a restoration of the land to the people of God.

To point to these changing circumstances is to focus upon historical events and their consequences, but not to move away from theology. The changes we have noted involve the theology of a people in transition. To point to historical bases of theological changes is not to suggest that the theological changes were simply opportunistic, for what we have here is an early example of the interaction of context and theology. Let it simply be noted here that the transition of context, from rural to urban in particular, is deeply embedded in the theology of our founding Scriptures. It is out of the change of context occasioned by the loss of nationhood and the severe challenge to hope in its restoration that a new theological style of thought emerged, that of apocalyptic.

2. THE EMERGENCE OF APOCALYPTIC

Apocalyptic sets the issue of the land in a new context, that of an impending overthrow of all earthly conditions in a fiery apocalypse. Central to apocalyptic is the notion of the kingdom of God, which will come into being in the destruction of the old kingdoms of the earth. In the visionary style of apocalyptic, earthly kingdoms are often referred to as "beasts" and set into schemes of periodization, as in this passage in Daniel.

> As for the fourth beast,
> there shall be a fourth kingdom on earth,
>   which shall be different from all the kingdoms,
> and it shall devour the whole earth,
>   and trample it down, and break it to pieces.
> As for the ten horns,
> out of this kingdom
>   ten kings shall arise,
>   and another shall arise after them;
> he shall be different from the former ones,
>   and shall put down three kings.
>
>   (7:23-24)

Puzzling as these references seem today, they were given quite specific political interpretations in the minds of those hearing them, pointing to the events that would lead up to the intervention of the Most High. In their rise to power the kingdoms of this earth challenge God by their words, by their treatment of the people of God, and by the unjust nature of their rule. When God acts, the action is one of judgment of that king who challenges the divine prerogative.

> But the court shall sit in judgment,
>   and his dominion shall be taken away,
>   to be consumed and destroyed to the end.
> And the kingdom and the dominion
>   and the greatness of the kingdoms under the whole heaven
>   shall be given to the people of the saints of the Most High;
> their kingdom shall be an everlasting kingdom,
>   and all dominions shall serve and obey them.
>
>   (Dan. 7:27)

The triumph of this new kingdom will be universal, and the people of the Most High will finally receive divine vindication for all that they have suffered. But the restoration of this kingdom naturally involves the return of their national territory. The land, although not mentioned in this text, is by implication promised to the people in their divine vindication.

At one time it was popular to interpret apocalyptic as a dualistic way of thought, which called for the destruction of all that is earthly in the name of the new heavenly reality. It is true that there is a heavenly or transcendent element in these sayings, but we must not exaggerate that aspect to the point where we miss the historical and geographical implications that are also present.[5] The tension between the heavenly and the earthly is visible in the book of Revelation.

> Then I saw a new heaven and a new earth; for the first heaven and the first earth had passed away, and the sea was no more. And I saw the holy city, new Jerusalem, coming down out of heaven from God, prepared as a bride adorned for her husband; and I heard a great voice from the throne saying, "Behold, the dwelling of God is with men. He will dwell with them, and they shall be his people, and God himself will be with them; he will wipe away every tear from their eyes, and death shall be no more, neither shall there be mourning nor crying nor pain any more, for the former things have passed away." (21:1-4)

Certainly the new Jerusalem transcends the old Jerusalem, and apocalyptic calls people to expect something from the hands of God that will transcend any past experience of earthly cities and earthly kingdoms. Still, the passage speaks of the new city coming out of heaven and of God's dwelling with them, the society of the faithful. It is speaking of a transformed and renewed existence that will be experienced *on this earth*. In the verses following, the images of the river of life and the tree of life call us back to the life of this earth and recall for us the scene of primal creation in Genesis 2:9-10. The new salvation to which the Apocalypse witnesses is paradisal in character, and as such it calls us back to the very foundation of the earth.[6] But paradise is understood here in terms of this earthly life.

To suggest that the theme of the land is dissolved in

apocalyptic would be a misstatement. The theme of the land continues in the apocalyptic writings, although in a qualified and perhaps muted way. In this regard apocalyptic has much in common with the earlier visions of Jewish eschatology, as recorded in Isaiah 2 and Micah 4.

> It shall come to pass in the latter days
> that the mountain of the house of the Lord
> shall be established as the highest of the mountains,
> and shall be raised up above the hills;
> and peoples shall flow to it. . . .
> They shall sit every man under his vine and under his fig tree,
> and none shall make them afraid.
>
> (Mic. 4:1-2, 4)

The prophecy of judgment of God is followed by a word about the peace that shall follow. That vision of peace, eschatological though it is, is related back to the land. To be sure, such talk is visionary. It looks forward in a prophetic way to a land yet to be enjoyed rather than to a land to be managed, in possession. But the direction of the visionary talk leads back to the land, land as agricultural resource. As part of the kingdoms delivered over to the people of God, the land is central. The dominion over all the kingdoms of the earth entails what Brueggemann aptly calls "new land arrangements."

In apocalyptic, as in much of Israel's prophetic eschatology, the future in the land is assumed to follow from God's blessing of God's righteous people. Even in the literature of the Qumran community the retreat to the wilderness is not undertaken for its own sake, nor to await the end of the earth. Rather, this retreat is an anticipation of the time when God will once again lead his faithful remnant into the land to possess it and to live off its abundance.[7] While these groups are not concerned with the practical details of managing the land, and while they may speak more of Jerusalem and the temple, the expectation of restoration to the land and its agricultural benefit is part and parcel of the expectation of God's vindicating intervention.

The New Testament is born on the knees of apocalyptic.[8] It is in the matrix of this intense expectation that the early Christian movement comes into being, and it is in the thought forms of apocalyptic that the earliest confessions of Christianity are couched. For the early Christians, then, the expectation of God's vindicatory intervention is uppermost. While mention of the land in this connection is rare in the New Testament, expectations abound relating to the land and to God's pleasure in giving it to those who do not possess. While less dramatic than the contents of apocalyptic visions, this presence of a land expectation cannot be dismissed. Thus Brueggemann is willing to interpret the Christian gospel in terms of the reversals of land loss and land gift.

We must face the fact, however, that it is not simply in terms of land that the New Testament texts speak of these expectations. What we see is a far bolder and more dramatic breakthrough. For the earliest Christians the kingdom of God has dawned in the presence of Jesus Christ himself. The power of the gospel for these Christians is that the event of Jesus Christ, and in particular his death and resurrection, represent the beginning of God's act of intervention. In Jesus Christ the kingdom is coming! In terms of Jewish expectation this Christian claim can only spell a crisis.

3. SHATTERING THE TERRITORIAL CHRYSALIS

The crisis in Jewish eschatology emerges from the claim that in Jesus Christ the kingdom of God has become a reality, experienced by his followers and disciples. What for Jewish apocalyptic lived in the realm of expectation now entered the Christian community as a matter of experience. While still living in hope of a future consummation, the Christians proclaimed that God's decisive intervention has already occurred. Of course, this did not mean the dissolution of all future aspects; indeed, expectation grew that Jesus would return within a generation and fulfill the remainder of the eschatological hopes of Israel. Apocalyptic lived on in the Christian community—the expectation of the return of Jesus is clearly an apocalyptic hope—but now it is centered in Jesus Christ. For Christians the whole range of hopes and expectations variously associated with Judaism must now be reinterpreted from the radical position "in Christ."

This meant that nothing was left the same. What hopes and expectations there might be for the restoration of the land to Israel must now be subject to Christ, and thus be open to reinterpretation. In the light of the overwhelming changes occurring in this event, we cannot be surprised that thought about the land would not be uppermost in the thoughts of the disciples. Yet the expectations of kingdom of God, already inaugurated, soon to be brought fully into existence, contained within them an expectation for the restoration of the land to God's people.

Divisions quickly sprang up within the Christian community, between the Jewish Christians and the Gentile Christians. While the former expected the traditional hope for the restoration of Israel to the land to be continued in Christian eschatology, the latter, more influenced by Hellenistic ideas, thought in more universal terms. While they did not deny the land component of the inherited apocalyptic thought, they tended to move it to the periphery of their thought. For them the central concern was that the Christian movement move out into all the world, in advance of the fulfillment of apocalyptic expectation. Here, then, is the center of the crisis for Jewish apocalyptic. Whereas in Jewish eschatology the kingdom of God would be first established on Mount Zion and then all the nations of the earth would flow to it, in the emerging Christian Hellenistic eschatology the gospel must first be preached to all nations, and then the kingdom would arrive (see Matt. 24:14; Mark 13:10; Luke 24:47; cf. Matt. 28:19).

The astonishing success of the mission to the Gentiles and the association with it of such a theological giant as Paul meant that the viewpoints of the Hellenistic Christians soon came to overshadow that of the Jewish Christians, although struggles persisted well into the second century. What this meant for Jewish expectation regarding the restoration of the land to Israel was clear to see. Davies puts it this way: "The Hellenists and Paul . . . broke asunder the territorial chrysalis of Christianity."[9] As the emerging Christian movement opened its wings, it was swept into a broad geographical context.

The effect of this was to encourage the movement already under way in postexilic Judaism of relativizing the sense of Jewish holy places. For the Christians too God was to be worshiped in the places in which they found themselves. Yet it is important to note that the holy places of Judaism continued to be important in Christian faith, only now as the places where Jesus lived, ministered, died, and was resurrected. In the emerging literature of the Christian movement the holy places are still taken seriously. Jesus weeps over Jerusalem, rides in glory into the city, prays in agony in a garden on Mount Olivet. For the burgeoning Christian movement these sites attain a spiritual importance from the fact of Jesus' presence in them. They are not intrinsically holy, but derive their holiness from the holiness of the one in whom the kingdom of God was seen to appear.

Still, the focus upon a particular piece of territory as the primary place for God's activity and the fulfillment of God's promise is forever broken. It seems we shall have to look elsewhere to find the hinge on which to hang the door of a New Testament theology of the land. For if the rapid extension of the Christian movement among the Gentiles had this strong effect on traditional expectations about holy places of Judaism, how much more did the fall of Jerusalem in 70 C.E. underline the emerging Christian notion that their faith could be tied to no single place.

We must now deal explicitly with the theological question involved in interpreting the New Testament in relation to our theme. W. D. Davies and Walter Brueggemann agree that the issue of land must be pursued in relation to the New Testament texts, but their opinions diverge sharply as to how that should be done and what results may be drawn from the inquiry. Brueggemann turns to a "land hermeneutic," while Davies offers a "christocentric reading."

For Brueggemann the dialectic of land loss and land gift that he has developed in the history of Israel becomes a tool by means of which the thrust of the New Testament writings can be understood and the theme of the land carried into the New Testament. Unwilling simply to concede that the New Testament "spiritualizes" the concrete emphases of the Old Testament on land, Brueggemann uses this dialectic to reflect on central gospel themes. In this analysis land loss and land gift point to the issues of dispossession and possession, issues that are clearly central to the New Testament dialectics, as witnessed, for example, in the song of Mary known as the Magnificat (Luke 1:46-55). By extension the dialectic of land loss and land gift can be used to interpret the central Pauline dialectic of law and grace. In effect, then, Brueggemann claims that land is a submerged but nevertheless present issue and theme in the New Testament. Its method of recovery is by a special hermeneutic.

In similar manner the apocalyptic vision of the new kingdom, the reversals of fortune that Jesus announces in the Sermon on the Mount as the hallmarks of the kingdom, and finally even the central events of the crucifixion and resurrection can all be understood through the prism of the land. Indeed, the dialectic of land loss/land gift comes to stand for Brueggemann as a metaphor for the central dialectic of the gospel. Between the landed and the landless stands the distinction between those who would grasp at power, status, and "turf," and thus will lose it, and those who possess no power, status, or "turf" and who are radically open to receive everything as a free gift. Land offers a hermeneutic correction, a theme that can "help us to discern dimensions of the text which could otherwise be overlooked."[10]

However, there are problems with Brueggemann's approach. By seeing the land as a metaphor for political realities and by using it as a hermeneutical concept for interpreting the New Testament, Brueggemann comes close to turning land into an abstract principle. In his concern to avoid theological spiritualization he runs the risk of a hermeneutical spiritualization. In doing this, Brueggemann passes over the concrete center of the New Testament witness and an important continuity between the two Testaments.

There is an essential continuity between God's activity in the election of Israel and the sending of Jesus Christ. As God has acted concretely to bless and save God's people in the history of Israel, so that work reaches a climax in Jesus Christ. From the point of view of the New Testament this continuity is clear. That God has acted concretely in Jesus Christ is testified by the form and the content of the New Testament. The event of Jesus Christ constitutes the center around which all else is organized. Thus Jesus Christ forms the point of continuity between God's activity in Israel and God's activity in the church.

At this point Davies' methodology provides a helpful counterpoint. Davies speaks in terms of an ambiguity in the New Testament with respect to the land. Different strata of tradition are preserved within the New Testament, and some strata are negative with respect to the land, while others see the land in positive light. There are those texts which reject the temple outright (Acts 7) and others which take the land, Jerusalem, and the temple up into a nongeographic, spiritual, transcendent dimension, where they become "symbols especially of eternal life, of the eschatological society in time and eternity, beyond space and sense."[11] There are also texts which regard the holy places in positive light. This is especially the case in the Gospels, where the need to locate Jesus in history carries with it the need to locate him geographically. As a real human person Jesus of Nazareth is a person inhabiting not only time but also space, not only history but also geography.

Where Davies is most helpful, I believe, is in seeing that both of these strata are shaped in their attitude to the land by the event of Jesus Christ. "Where Christianity has reacted seriously to the *realia* of Judaism, whether negatively or positively, it has done so in terms of Christ, to whom all places and all space, like all things else, are subordinated."[12] In both the breaking down of Jewish territorial expectation and the fashioning of a new understanding of holy place and apocalyptic expectation, the New Testament witnesses to its focus upon Jesus Christ. It has, in Davies' term, "Christified holy space." The christification of holy space indicates both the substitution of the holiness of the person for the holiness of a place and, by extension, the process whereby new places became holy by virtue of their association with Christ. The term points to a transformation of received notions of space by the event of Jesus Christ.

Finally, we must link this development with the suggestion that the New Testament spiritualizes the Jewish emphasis on the land. It seems that Brueggemann has developed his land hermeneutic to avoid this tendency. Davies, too, considers that a whole stratum of New Testament material, including the apocalyptic material, treats the land negatively by spiritualizing it or by rendering it transcendent. As the discussion of apocalyptic has indicated, it is clear that apocalyptic expectation does maintain a firm rootage in actual history and geography, for all its modification of them. It is false to consider this a "spiritualization." The language of apocalyptic contains very down-to-earth implications in conjunction with its transcendent component. If, as I have suggested, apocalyptic carries on the hope for the land, then these texts, albeit in a qualified and transposed way, may carry a positive significance for the theme of land.

The focusing of Christian expectation in Jesus Christ must not be understood as a spiritualizing or a transcendentalizing. In Jesus Christ the concreteness of God's activity with Israel comes to a particular focus. For the early Christians, Jesus Christ is no abstraction, removed from earthly existence. Indeed, their faith proclaims that it is in their down-to-earth living that the risen Christ encounters them in the Spirit. Thus the emphasis on Christ does not dissolve or spiritualize the concrete emphasis of the Old Testament, but rather deepens and extends it. For christification of holy space traces the continuation of a pattern already apparent in Judaism, in which the locus of God's saving activity is simultaneously narrowed and, in principle, made more inclusive: from the land to Jerusalem, the temple to Mount Zion, and, finally, from each of these to the person of Jesus Christ.

While the focus on Jesus Christ represented a potential break with Judaism, the movement that followed in many ways paralleled movements with respect to the land and to holy place already present in Judaism. Davies points to a deepening awareness of personal religious experience which in some ways also deflected interest away from the land. He speaks of "an undeniable relocation of interest away from The Land to *the broadly* human."[13] Postexilic Judaism's focus on personal experience and the broadly human is certainly different from the extensive christocentrism of the Christian movement. But in the focus upon the human and the human experience of God—for the Jews in the Torah, for the Christians in the Holy Spirit—we find important parallels.

The extension of the mission to the Gentiles also has parallels in the Jewish experience of diaspora. According to Baruch Bokser, "The early rabbinic system, recognizing the potential for sacredness in the whole world, taught that extra-Temple sacredness needs to be activated."[14] For both movements notions of holy space are extended; the territorial chrysalis is broken in many ways. For both Jew and Christian it becomes a matter of personal experience that God can be known and worshiped in places far removed from God's holy temple in Jerusalem. Clearly it is not that the sense of holy space is simply universalized, but rather that the people of faith find God is with them in the places they find themselves.

In the changing times of postexilic Judaism and the emergence of the early Christian movement powerful forces are at work to reshape the understanding of God's engagement with space and place. For both Jews and Christians new understandings which speak of great extension of God's presence emerge. Yet in important ways the old emphasis upon God's special relationship with special places receives new impetus. If the theme of land as such disappears, the stress upon the transformation of space "in Christ" and in the presence of the kingdom of God is highlighted in the New Testament. Further, the doctrine of the Incarnation which emerges in early christological reflection within the Christian community offers a powerful new motive to relate God with chosen space once again.

But before we can trace that development, we must turn our attention to the fate of the notions of place and space in the development of the philosophical tradition in which Christian theology was to receive its first definitive form. If the seeds for a continuation and development of the special relationship of the God of Jesus Christ with particular places are to be found in the Christian Scriptures, it must immediately be admitted that those seeds were to fall on rather barren ground.

CHAPTER FOUR

The Poetics of Space: Place and Space in the Western Tradition

One of the reasons for the lack of a strong theology of the land lies with the predominant emphases of the Western philosophical tradition. This tradition has tended to move issues of place to the very periphery of philosophical reflection. Our task in this chapter is to substantiate this claim, and to suggest ways in which the deficit might be made up.

1. THE TRIUMPH OF HOMOGENEOUS SPACE

In common speech we distinguish space from place by regarding the first as the general inclusive category and the second as that which defines specific locations within space. This accords with the classical view of space, which emerged in the seventeenth and eighteenth centuries and which understood space as a featureless, homogeneous void. The classical view still shapes popular thinking about space and place, although it is important to realize that the concepts have not always been related in this way. Indeed, this classical view is at odds with earlier views and with the understanding that emerges from contemporary physics, informed by the theories of relativity and quantum mechanics.

Space itself may be defined in terms of place(s). In the thought of the Aboriginal people of Australia, for example, the world is constituted as a series of places connected to one another by the tracks of the Dreamtime heroes. An Aboriginal understands space in terms of the network of sacred sites that constitute his world and orient him in relation to it. According to Salomon Bochner, the earliest Hebrew and Greek notions of space were notions of place, *makom* in Hebrew, *topos* in Greek.[1] Place is not conceived as a mere point, a location, but as an arena which partakes of the qualities of that which dwells there. Places are themselves identifiable, can be said to have qualities and meanings.

In Aboriginal mythology it is the place which lends meaning to the stories. If you have heard a piece of mythology but not "seen the place," the Aborigines believe you cannot understand, let alone believe, the sacred story. In Hebrew religion we find that place names have special significance, lending their qualities to events that occurred there. Thus Jacob meets God at Luz when he fled from his brother, and he returns there later to meet God again and to purify himself and his people. The significance of this place as the meeting place with God is carried into the new name that Jacob gives it, Bethel (Gen. 35).

Hebrew thought stresses the terrestrial sphere as the location of God's dealings with humanity. But even in Hebrew thought place has a cosmological nuance, pointing to the world beyond our daily affairs. In Genesis 1, for example, God gathers the waters under the heavens into *one place* so that the dry land appeared. God too has a dwelling place, which is designated *makom,* and this term sometimes comes to stand for God. It is in Greek thought, however, that the cosmological nuances of place are developed into systematic cosmologies. In this development the beginnings of the transition to the classical notion of space are seen.

In early Greek thought a variety of understandings are present. For some, such as Lucretius, space is the infinite container of all that occurs. For others space is finite, a material entity like air, and is the medium in which all other things take their places. Aristotle's concept of space as the adjacent boundary of the containing body is essentially a concept of place. As developed in the *Physics* this view avoids both the material view and the idea of infinite space. However, it stresses the essential emptiness and character-less quality of space.

Aristotle's concept of a finite enclosure has relevance both for physics and for cosmology. It can be applied to the space of earthly and heavenly bodies. But, it should be stressed that Aristotle, like Plato, maintains a distinction between the vast cosmological space of the heavens and earthly places. Whereas place *(topos)* is used for the space of human scale, another word, *chora,* is used to speak of the wider, undefined space.[2] In this regard Aristotle's view of space prefigures that of contemporary physics with its different concepts of space for different levels of organization. However, the notions of space that were disseminated by Hellenism lacked Aristotle's subtlety. Here it was ideas such as the finite medium or the infinite container that gained currency. Each stressed the idea of space as an empty void, characterless and without qualities, which could be applied to both terrestrial and celestial spaces. In these Greek notions we find the foundations of the classical notion of homogeneous space.

If the earliest views of space preserve the scale of terrestrial places, the same cannot be said for the classical physics that emerges from the work of Newton and Descartes. Newton conceives of one vast, uniform space, in which laws of motion are consistent. His brilliant connection of the falling apple with the movement of heavenly bodies according to the law of gravitation links the terrestrial and the celestial realms in one vast, uniform space. For Newton, God is the infinite receptacle, so that space and time have an absolute status as attributes of God independent of material bodies.[3] In this system space is defined by a series of fixed, or relatively fixed, coordinate axes.[4]

This concept forms a transition between the notion of a

material space and the mathematical views of space which triumph in the modern period. Understood as the body of God, Newtonian space has substance and character, but understood as mathematical space defined by axes, it is empty, homogeneous, and characterless. The sense of the inherent qualities of place is lost when the transition is made to the generalized notion of space.

The move toward space as homogeneous void received impetus from the work of Descartes, especially in the dualism he established between mind and matter. By seeing reality as composed of two fundamentally different types of existents, matter and mind, extended beings and thinking beings (*res extensa* and *res cogitans*), Descartes drew a fundamental distinction between human reality and mere physical reality. Once human reality was bracketed off from physical reality, the way was open to reduce physical reality to mere material reality, and the new materialism of the scientific age was effectively launched. In this view space is characterized only by extension, and thus is material.

On the other side, Descartes's elevation of the thinking substance, humanity, had the theological effect of emphasizing the human at the expense of the natural. If nature was not thinking substance, then theology need give it little attention. God, of course, was thinking substance, and so it followed that God's concern lay more with that section of reality which shared God's capacity for thought and thus bore God's own image. By grouping humanity and God over against nature, Descartes strengthened tendencies already present to devalue nature, both religiously and scientifically. The objectification of nature which enabled the formation of the natural sciences at the same time fueled an attitude of religious indifference to nature.[5]

The homogeneous void of the emerging concept of space is further identified as passive in Descarte's metaphysic. Although empty, space is still a species of matter, and as such it is devoid of the centers of activity found in the thinking substances. The empty expanse of space is now characterized as without purpose or initiative. Human interest in space can only lie in its mapping and its utilization. Soon we arrive at the view that the human role is to take the empty, featureless space and "make something of it." The presumption of this view still prevails in popular thought today, and is one of the foundations of our disregard for the integrity of nature and the intrinsic and unique qualities of places. All may be reduced to the one geometric vision.

It is fascinating to note that developments in contemporary physics overthrow the classical notions about space and draw us back to something that is closer to the Aristotelean place. Contemporary physics, informed by the theories of relativity and quantum mechanics, no longer sees a uniform space ruled by laws of universal consistency. It is necessary now to distinguish the realms of space. In the middle level, defined by human scale, Newtonian physics still seems to work, which perhaps accounts for the persistence of the classical view in popular thinking. But at the quantum level Heisenberg's indeterminacy principle applies, so that measurement and definiteness become extremely elusive. Here we are in a "statistical space" in which the understandings of quantum mechanics draw us away from Newtonian thought.

In measurements relating to our galaxy, however, we must think in terms of yet another sort of space in which Einstein's general theory of relativity prevails. Today if we want to know what space is, we must first determine the scale of the inquiry: are we speaking of the quantum level or the galactic, and so on? In some ways we may say that space is once again being defined by place. The notion of scale, banished from physics by Newton, seems to be emerging once again as a key consideration.

Yet if space is to be understood as discrete levels of organization, this does not mean that we are moving toward a more fragmented view of reality. Rather, as David Bohm has argued, we are drawn in the other direction, toward wholeness, for another fundamental of quantum mechanics is that the distinction between the observer and the observed is no longer absolute. "Rather both observer and observed are merging and interpenetrating aspects of one whole reality, which is indivisible and unanalysable."[6] Our thought cannot be taken as a description of the world as it is so much as a partial vision of it. It must see itself as part of a totality of which we, the thinkers, are part. By contrast, fragmentary thinking is part of the atomistic view, which understands reality as composed of aggregates of atoms.

Further, in the emerging physics the hold of materialism is being broken. Upon examination matter does not appear to be the solid, abiding substance it has traditionally been held to be. Attention is some quarters is moving toward mind or consciousness as that which is the really real. In all this the rigid dichotomy of Descartes is beginning to break down. A change from our traditional ways of viewing reality, especially natural and spatial reality, is well under way in contemporary physics, although it has yet to filter its way into common thought and speech.

The move toward a new way of viewing reality in which the human does not stand over against the natural and spatial is fundamental to the argument of this book. We shall find further intimations of this new perceptual style when we examine Gaston Bachelard's "poetics of space." This method will enable us to recapture the terrestrial and human scale of topography, which was lost in the scientific enthusiasm of the development of classical physics. Yet in very significant ways homogeneous space was not able to banish place completely.

2. THE PERSISTENCE OF PLACE

The developments in quantum mechanics are just one of the ways in which the issues of place and its relation to human being have returned to haunt modern and postmodern society. If we turn to the voices of contemporary literature, we find a constant theme of the human person living in a void, without home, without a sense of direction, without a place. In our time we find ourselves uprooted, without a sense of belonging anywhere. These cultural indicators should not be dismissed. Further, developments within the human sciences bear out the impression that there is something deeply rooted in our humanity which seeks to know itself in terms of place.

In the last two decades a new discipline of social or humanistic geography has emerged. Growing out of the traditional discipline of geography, this discipline seeks to understand human variables and to correlate insights from the human sciences, sociology and psychology, with more narrowly geographical knowledge. One of the more interesting parts of this endeavor traces the social and individual effects of different styles of rural and urban planning. These very styles can be traced back to various conceptions of space. As the scope of the sciences broadens to include the human sciences, the far-reaching implications of our concepts of space can be traced.

A social geographer who has done very significant work in this area is Anne Buttimer. According to Buttimer an essential element of personal identity and health is place identity. Characteristic of all earth life forms, place identity refers to the need for self-definition in terms of both a "home place" and a "horizon of reach." We need a secure home place for a base and shelter and to provide spatial security. Also we need a familiar area of reach, over which we may freely move to meet other survival needs, such as food, social contact, ritual activity. In this fundamental need humans are no different from animals. But the human difference lies in the ability to become aware of these factors and by means of social planning to alter the balances inhering in the simple dialectics of home and reach.[7]

In the period since the Second World War, Buttimer sees the outworking of an Einsteinian view of space and spatial relationships. This view deemphasizes place for the sake of centralization and rationalization. Such examples as the development of multinational corporations and the spread of international franchises in everything from auto mufflers to health care open up the sense of the global reach and relativity of all things. Regional and local distinctiveness tends to be lost in this process. Further, a multinational corporation subsumes all particular places, such as mines, fields, and forests, under the profit motive of a centralized and integrated structure. In Einstein's terms, then, the global relativity of all space and time dissolves the reality of place. At the level of urban and rural planning we see a dissolution of local markets with local products, and throughout our entire society we see examples of the multinational, multi-investment corporations. Coca-Cola is truly a worldwide enterprise, and makes that point in its own advertising: "I'd like to buy the world a Coke."

Now we can see the entire environmental issue in the broader context of changes in the ways in which we see and shape our world. The loss of a sense of place is built into the forces of postmodern development. Buttimer puts it this way: "The skyscrapers, airports, freeways, and other stereotypical components of modern landscapes—are they not the sacred symbols of a civilization which has deified reach and derided home?"[8] At the time when we have expanded reach to embrace the entire globe, we have undermined the distinctiveness and reality of home places. In creating "placeless landscapes of reach," modern rural and urban planning has uprooted what reminders there were of a sense of the local and unique, except where these can be packaged and marketed for national and, if possible, international consumption.

The losses we face here are more than emotional; they are matters of health and identity. Health and identity are both severely threatened by the uprooting of persons from places. Without a sense of place—the essential basis for the definition of both home place and horizon of reach—there can be no centering of the human psyche. "Personal identity and health require an ongoing process of centering—a reciprocity between dwelling and reaching—which can find its external symbolic representation in the sense of place or regional identity."[9] As members of contemporary society we encounter many impediments to the development of a sense of place and the sort of centering that our psyches seem naturally to desire. The movement of our history has been in the other direction.

From the outset Hellenistic sophistication regarded such faiths as that of the Hebrews in God's special relation to a particular land, a city, and a temple as relics of archaic nonsense, the relevance of which are exploded by the more general, and thus more "correct," views of space. Reinforced in the age of science, the generalized view of space was subject to mathematical interpretation, with the effect of moving the concept of space beyond the grasp of the average person. The persistence of the classical notion of space as an infinite, homogeneous void has worked together with the loss of a sense of qualitative local place. In our own time the beginning of space travel, on however modest a scale, further reinforces thinking of space in the most general and expansive of terms.

Yet the deep irony of all this is that our very terrestrial existence is becoming problematical. Just at the time the general and extraterrestrial views of space seem to have triumphed, we experience a crisis both culturally and ecologically in our relations with earthly space. The trivializing of the earthly and topographical features of human existence seems to lie at the root of our contemporary crises, both personal and ecological. Today we are reaping the dubious benefits of that view of space which trivializes the earthly and the human dimension of existence. Without retreating to archaic thought forms it nevertheless is incumbent upon us to recover something of the Hebrew understanding of place if we are to avoid ecological disaster.

However, our presentation would be one-sided if it ended here. If the Christian faith has lost its hold upon the Hebrew sense of sacred places and land as gift, and if modern philosophy, economics, and regional planning act concertedly to undermine the all-important sense of place, are there not countervailing forces? To be sure! In the literature of uprooted peoples we discover strong intimations of the rediscovery of a sense of place in areas far removed from the home countries. Examples could be furnished from the postcolonial literature of Australia and North America, as well as many other nations. These literary examples could be joined by others from the visual arts—from painting, photography, and film. I would propose that the arena of the aesthetic may hold vital clues for that rediscovery of place. It is with this possibility in mind that we can consider work of Gaston Bachelard in developing the "poetics of space." Set alongside the move toward contextualization in theology, the poetics of space will offer us the methodology we need to fashion an incarnational theology of place.

3. THE POETICS OF SPACE

In Bachelard's work we find the beginnings of a method of aesthetics which can assist us in recovering the sense of place. Bachelard proposes that attention to this aesthetic offers us a way to avoid the reductive inheritance of our philosophical tradition that has rendered all space geometric and homogeneous. As a philosopher of science he is well aware of the methodological problems posed by the Western philosophical tradition in relation to the perception of space. "With space images," he writes, "we are in a region where reduction is easy, commonplace."[10]

Calling himself a "philosopher of the adjective," Bachelard seeks to avoid the substantialist bias of Western philosophy whereby we think only things or substances are real. He wants to direct our attention to the qualities of places and spaces. Hence his interest in adjectives, for adjectives speak of qualities and properties. Even more, Bachelard calls our attention to the image, for the image, like the adjective, signifies qualities. In line with some of the insights of the new physics Bachelard will not accept any simple disjunction between the objective and the subjective. He will not accept the familiar philosophical prejudice that finds the adjectival elements "subjective" and the thing itself "objective." This form of dualism is at the root of modern problems in the perception of the environment. Bachelard draws our attention to poetic images, for he maintains that the adjectival image affords us access to the prereflective unity of subject and object, and thus establishes a firmer basis for a true knowledge of both humanity and nature.

Bachelard speaks evocatively of our need to open our perceptual windows to the richness of poetic imagery. All too often we dismiss the image with the rational question: What does it mean? In place of this reductionism Bachelard urges us to let the image stand, to reverberate in all its newness. For the poetic image is always novel in its approach to us; it represents a "flare-up of being" in the imagination and is "the sign of new being." Its effect on us must be allowed—Bachelard speaks of learning to vibrate in response to the image. By giving our whole attention to the poetic image, by resisting the reductive modes of perception our philosophical tradition has taught us, we will be able to perceive the true reality of the places we encounter.

Bachelard claims nothing less than that through images places will find voice. The environment may "speak" to us in a new and renewing language if we resist the reductive ways of seeing. If we give attention to the poetic images coined of various places, we will be able to cease seeing places as featureless "things" and begin to notice their qualities. In this way we will be more able to resist the massive reduction of the "development" and "extractive" mythologies. Further, in the poetic image the foundations of our own being will be laid bare, for the image, Bachelard claims, is of ontological significance. Here we find echoes of the later Heidegger, who called for a new mode of apprehension in the face of the sheer "isness" of being. Heidegger's *Gelassenheit* and Bachelard's space for reverie and day-dream have much in common. Bachelard, like Heidegger, is prescribing a new way of listening, a form of meditative thought in which place will disclose itself, gripping and overcoming human persons in their essential condition.[11]

If Eliade demonstrated the ontological significance of sacred space for religious humanity, Bachelard demonstrates the ontological significance of felicitious space for postmodern humanity. In *The Poetics of Space* the close link between the places one inhabits and the development of identity and depth of personhood is again and again demonstrated. With Heidegger, Bachelard is saying, "Look again." Look again at the familiar, at that which you take for granted, at what seems like nothing to you. Here you will find beauty and ugliness, fullness and emptiness. In this disclosure your own being will be apprehended; you will find yourself already moving out into space and retracting into yourself, renewed or aroused to withdrawal. Just as human being is flexible, so space is charged with qualities, is able to shape and transform us as we come to know it and enter into relationship with it.[12]

How can the methodology of phenomenological poetics assist us in our theological task? First, it will suggest a new locus for our theological foundations. Instead of turning only to the formulated ideas of our philosophical tradition, we must now turn to the images that shape our very being. In relation to a theology of the land images of place, of land of sea, must be ingredient in our theological reflection. Second, the use of poetics can suggest ways in which theology can become truly contextual in its methods. Contextuality implies plurality in the shaping of theological thinking. Here attention to the image can be of great significance, for, by their very nature, images are nonexclusive. One image does not exclude another, but image invites counterimage, and insight develops out of a plurality of apparently divergent sets of imagery. Methodologically this means that theology must surrender one-dimensional notions of truth and traditional structures of logic. This is by no means an invitation to enter into chaos and witness the end of theology. Rather, it will mean a new appreciation of the coherence of images and the logics of implication and intuition, which have been widely ignored in traditional theological methodology.

Finally, poetics offers a new way of seeing, a new way of thinking. If persons could be brought to "see" places, and to find their own being in dialectical relation with the space they occupy, a powerful force would be released for the care of the earth. Images grow out of the concrete experience of a people, their suffering, their sense of their environment. It is through images that the environment can gain a voice. To be sure, images are human products and, as such, are integrated into human ways of being and perceiving. But, as Bachelard suggests, through the image an access is gained to a prereflective unity of human and nonhuman. In poetic images we express both ourselves and our environment. The image then is valuable in the task of contextualizing theology, for through the image we gain access to human experience of its locality. The human spirit is invoked in response to its environment.

Only when we are able to respond to landscapes, whether those of earth's pristine beauty or those that portray the harmonious interplay of human activity and natural resources, will the foundations be laid for a renewal of theological reflection on the land. It is this mode of perception which circumvents the geometric sensibility and other reductions of space and opens up for us a new way of seeing again the old familiar places, which will enable us to think in creative theological ways about the rural, urban, or suburban spaces that surround us and call for our care. Following Bachelard, I propose that a theology that gives fundamental attention to the poetic image is on the way to the reshaping required of contextual theology.[13]

4. IMAGES AND THE CONTEXTUALIZATION OF THEOLOGY

The methodological turn of Bachelard's poetics of space has important links with the contextualization of theology. As our study of Cox and Brueggemann has suggested, and our attention to Aboriginal and Hebrew religion has reinforced, theology today must be contextual and address a variety of contexts. It is here that attention to the image may be most helpful. A theology that draws its foundations from the images of a local context—images of desire, of struggle, identification, and suffering—will not confuse its contextual normativity with some abstract universalism. A theology that grows out of local images will not be dismayed by the plurality of *possible* contexts, for it will be bound to the concreteness of the *actual* location. It is only out of the "poetics of contextualization" that a true theology of context can emerge. The importance of the people's images is widely recognized in many Third World theologies. The increasing awareness of the importance of images in theology to a large extent grows out of the emerging contextual character of contemporary theology.

It is significant that those theologians who are beginning to explore the theology of images are most notably spokespersons for groups that have traditionally been denied a voice in theological formulation: women, blacks, members of developing countries. Thus we find great attention to images in feminist theology, black theology, and Minjung theology. A powerful example is provided by C. S. Song's *Theology from the Womb of Asia*. Here we see concerns of minority peoples who suffer and images of the environment coming together. Indeed, it is in the poetry of a people that the deepest connections are forged between human suffering and the presence of their environment.

Song quotes the poetry of the Kalinga people of the Philippines:

> If the land could speak,
> It would speak for us,
> It would say, like us, that the years
> Have forged the bond of life that ties us together.
> It was our labour that made the land what she is.
> And it was her yielding that gave us life.
> We and the land are one![14]

Here we see human suffering growing out of identification with local environment, the fusion of human passion with the land. It is this passion which begets the fusions of poetry. It is this passion which produces the resonance of the human voice, whether it is raised in song or in theology.

Song uses an analysis of the character and qualities of the Japanese poetic form *haiku* to illustrate this quality of resonance, or *hibiki*. *Hibiki*, literally echo, is the quality of resonance possessed by poetic utterance. It is something of the quality of passion that we find in other poetic or parabolic statements, which speak from the depths of human experience.

"*Haiku* is the *hibiki* of life. It is the echo of history in the grip of destiny. And it is the resonance of the world in the presence of the powers that affect it."[15] This resonance is not simply a reflection of human inwardness; it is a resonance of the world, and it grows out of the interaction of the humanity and the surrounding world.

Like works of art theology that is true to its context should possess *hibiki,* resonance. Looking at Jesus, Song finds one whose teaching has resonance and therefore touches the life of the common people. This is because Jesus' theology emerged from the *hibiki* he heard and felt in his own life and the life of others. In Song's view, Jesus is a "nature theologian," experiencing deeply the presence of the natural environment, which presses daily upon the experience of the common people in their suffering and their celebration. The parables of Jesus, with their wealth of local, environmental, and homespun images, speak to the depths of the human condition.

Likewise it is through the images of such people as the Kalinga that Asian theologians can begin to voice a theology that will speak to the depths of Asian people. A theology without *hibiki*—and this is how Western theology appears in Asian eyes—has no power to speak to the human heart, whether it is a Hindu heart, a Buddhist heart, or a Confucianist heart. Counterfeit theology, like counterfeit poetry, fails at the bar of the resonance of its language and its syntax, as Isaiah suggested in 28:10. Song applies this verse to our theology and our time.

If our theology does not reflect in some way God's grammar, if it does not arise from the syntax of the suffering and longing heart, and if it is not the semantics that touches the agonizing and hoping soul, then our theology is still unintelligible. It is still a theology of precept upon precept and line upon line.[16]

If theology is called in these times to take heed of its context, it is also, and at the same time, pulled in the direction of giving attention to the local images which mirror context.

Returning to our Western contexts, it is apparent that we have moved far from such a passionate relationship with our environment. Theologically we have tended to interpret context only in terms of historical experience and to gloss over the experience of place. This is obviously of a piece with the developments in Western philosophy and science which we have traced. Less obvious but just as telling is the actual alienation we have experienced from the localities we occupy. Again, Song: "It is a great pity that modern civilization strongly alienates us from the land. . . . We are supposed to belong to the earth, but we live far above it, detached and separated from it. Perhaps this is one of the reasons why many of us feel homeless."[17] It is this alienation that has brought us to the brink of environmental disaster. And it is this alienation which a theology of the land must centrally address and heal.

In drawing attention to these factors we are not seeking to spearhead a romantic movement "back to the land." Such a supposed solution is not only elitist but fundamentally wrongheaded. Its results are, all too often, the displacement of rural poor by urban rich and the displacement of working land by recreational land. The gentrification of rural belts surrounding urban centers serves only the gratification of those who can afford to buy a weekend place; the net effect is to withdraw more and more acres from active and useful agriculture.[18] True environmentalism, like charity, begins at home. In the immediate locality of our work and our residence we must find the place that we would serve and save. For Christians the locality of work or residence most naturally coincides with the locality for worship and service.

And Christian theology, in its drive to become contextualized to the localities in which faith is alive, must seek to know the places in which it is found.

To be true to its Hebrew roots and to be responsive to the challenges of expanding contextualization, theology must embrace the spirits of the localities in which it arises. The historical message of Christianity must be read geographically by means of the images of place out of which its practitioners shape their lives. In so doing it will not betray some universality imagined by many as its birthright; rather, it will embrace faithfully what is an essential element of its incarnational foundation. If God became human in Jesus Christ, as Christianity has always maintained, then God became human in a particular time and *a particular place*. In seeking a theology which is local, that is, a theology which develops the images of the local context, we are doing no more than calling for a truly incarnational theology.

CHAPTER FIVE

The Christification of Holy Space: Incarnation and the Land

In the previous chapter we called for an incarnational theology that would develop out of images of the local context. Such, we suggested, would be the proper method for an ecological theology based in the notion of place. If the methodology for ecological theology is contextual and uses the "poetics of contextualization," the substance of an ecological theology is the Incarnation of God.

The event of Jesus Christ is the center from which all else in Christian faith radiates. As we shape the theology of the land, it is important to bear in mind that where we locate our center shapes fundamentally the substance of the theology we develop. For this reason the event of Jesus Christ needs to provide the center and focus of Christian theology of the land. Such a center reflects the ordering of biblical faith, which historically proceeds from the knowledge of God as redeemer to knowledge of God as creator. The desire to reflect the logic of the Christian tradition leads us to center our presentation in the Incarnation. Paul Santmire comments that any attempt to develop a theology of nature will have to go down "to the deepest roots of Western religious sensibility and vocabulary," if it is to plumb the depths of the ambiguity we find there in respect to nature and come up to speak with a clear voice out of the tradition.[1] Theologies of the earth which work only with creation or natural theology fail this test. By ignoring the redemptive and incarnational elements, they fail to engage the deepest roots of Christian faith.

Further, there is a concern to acknowledge the dire situation in which we find ourselves in relation to our environment, and this concern draws us in the theological direction of the Incarnation. John Hart recently has suggested that with regard to the environment we do not stand at a crossroads, where we can pause and make a simple choice between the two pathways, the one the way of life and the other the way of death. Already we have gone far down the pathway of death which leads to the despoilation and destruction of our environment.[2] It is no longer a matter of free choice whether to choose life or death. We are already far down the way of death, and the issue is whether we will turn back from this way and then seek another. It is, in fact, a matter of repentance and conversion. As we view the challenges facing us in the next twenty years, we need not merely wisdom but redemption, not an adjustment of course but a fundamental change of heart. The urgency of our need prompts us to make straight for the center of Christian faith, the narrative of the Savior, the event of the Incarnation. For it is there, we have learned, that conversion of heart is the agenda.

Incarnation is the locus of God's decisive self-revelation and thus is the point from which God's relationship to the created order can best be manifested. It is the crowning point of concreteness, which fulfills earlier indications of the ways of God with God's people. In particular, it fulfills and transforms the earlier emphasis upon the land as the content of God's favor to God's people. Jesus Christ is the fulfillment of the elements of concreteness in God's dealing with the people of Israel, the land, the temple, and the city set on the holy mount. Each of these finds its completion and reference in Jesus Christ, who is the Yes of all the promises of God.

Finally, the Incarnation has deep significance for a

Christian understanding of space and time. Understood as the creator of space and time, God is distinct and separate from space and time. As the Incarnate One, God enters into the deepest possible relationship with space and time. In the Incarnation we consider God's fundamental engagement with space and time, an engagement which can leave nothing the same, no stone unturned. It is in this engagement of God with our place and our time that we must anchor our hope for the possible future of the earth.

1. JESUS AND THE LAND

As a Jew living in the first century Jesus naturally had a special relationship to the land of Palestine. He was heir to the long tradition of promise and expectation whereby the Jews waited for God to restore them to the land first promised to Abraham. Yet there was something special about Jesus' relationship to the land. I want in the course of this section to make it clear that the special quality of Jesus' relation to the land was not a matter of political expectations, but something far more subtle and profound.

Still, the prevalence of a political expression at the time of Jesus' life and ministry must be acknowledged. Groups such as the Zealots were contemplating an uprising against the Romans that would return the land to the Jewish people. Attempts to understand Jesus in the light of these movements have a long history. An early understanding of Jesus' messiahship held that Jesus would be the one to restore the land to the children of Israel. This view was not borne out by the experience of Jesus' passion. In recent times others have argued that Jesus belonged to a group like the Zealots and himself harbored expectations about political deliverance.

Reviewing this evidence, W. D. Davies concludes that Jesus was not a Zealot and indeed, "paid little attention to the relationship between Yahweh, and Israel and the land." The movement which Jesus started certainly had its revolutionary aspects, but the overthrow of Rome was not a part of it. Rather, Jesus sought to establish a new kind of community among the Jewish people which would be marked by radically new understandings of the law and of the relationships between leaders and people and between men and women. According to Davies, "The aim of Jesus was neither non-political nor directly political: rather, it was focused on the creation of a community worthy of the name of the people of God within Israel."[3]

This conclusion is shared by Karl Barth, who finds in Jesus a remarkable freedom in relation to the institutions of the family, the state, and the law courts. For example, in saying "Render to Caesar the things that are Caesar's and to God the things that are God's," Jesus was refusing to oppose the Romans' right to taxation but at the same time refusing to confuse the right of tribute with the demand for loyalty to God. This is what Barth calls Jesus' "lordly freedom." It seems that in relation to the burning political issues of the land Jesus exercised a lordly freedom, neither condoning the Roman overlordship nor calling for its overthrow.

It would be a mistake, however, to imply from this that Jesus' ministry, and in particular his proclamation of the kingdom of God, did not have its political and economic consequences. In Jesus' refusal to back a particular political program we must not find an apolitical message. Barth and Davies clearly avoid this mistake. So too would it be wrong to find in Jesus' refusal to endorse a particular version of the relationship between God, nation, and land an indication that the special relationship between God's covenant and the land is somehow annulled in Jesus' proclamation. We must exercise more care if we are to trace the connections with the necessary precision.

There is another whole aspect of relationship to the land to which we have often referred in this book. We have seen it in the Australian Aborigines and we have seen it in the special relationships people of different cultures have developed to their own locality. It is the intimate link between a person's life and the person's environment, the linking of the inner and outer worlds which finds expression in the images that person uses to describe the environment and the experience of life. The preceding chapter outlined the method of the "poetics of space" that Gaston Bachelard used to develop features of the special aesthetic relationship which people develop to the places and spaces of their lives. Could the methods of poetics be applied to the teachings of Jesus to sound out his special relationship to the land in which he lived?

One scholar who points us in this direction is C. S. Song. Song sees a parallel between the sayings of Jesus and the *haiku* of the Japanese poet Basho. He presents the saying of Jesus in *haiku* form:

> Look at the birds of the air;
> they do not sow and reap and store in barns.
>
> Your heavenly Father feeds them.
> You are worth more than the birds! [Matt. 6:26]

Song remarks: "Jesus hits on something—birds of the air, the birds fed by God. The hitting produces *hibiki,* echoing back to Jesus and his listeners: you are worth more than they!"[4]

In finding the quality of *hibiki,* or resonance, in the words of Jesus, Song is pointing to an aspect of Jesus' ministry that is only now coming into clear focus—his sensibility, the natural and characteristic use of aesthetic forms in his sayings. This quality of Jesus' ministry has far-reaching implications for the quest of the historical Jesus.[5] Without wishing to resurrect the effort to penetrate the consciousness of Jesus, I think we are on the threshhold of new insight into the sensibility that speaks through the sayings of Jesus.

As part of this effort our own enquiry here can focus upon the relationship to the environment suggested by a careful reading of the sayings of Jesus. Song proposes that Jesus "is a nature theologian of the first rank!" While this may be exaggerating the case, it is clear that Jesus possessed a profound sense of the natural environment and lived in an intimate relationship with natural forces and environmental realities. Consider:

> Love your enemies and pray for those who persecute you, so that you may be sons of your Father who, is in heaven; for he makes his sun rise on the evil and on the good, and sends rain on the just and on the unjust. (Matt. 5:44-45)

Contrast this reference to the sun and the rain with our twentieth-century sensibility. Would we not see in the facts Jesus quotes some indication of the indifference of nature, the blind and amoral workings of natural law? Jesus sees quite the opposite. Faced with the fact that sun shines and rain falls without regard for persons or ethical niceties, Jesus sees a metaphor for the grace of the Father. The truly radical ethical injunction to love one's enemies is supported by an appeal to the indiscriminate care that God gives to all creatures through the faithfulness of the natural environment.

We could speak at length about the connections, ethical and theological, to be drawn from this saying. But let us simply observe that for Jesus the sun and the rain are direct witnesses to the nature of God. Note that he is not mounting an argument for God's faithfulness or developing a natural theology. Jesus is not interested in such theological refinements, but has a more urgent and vital concern. He is calling his listeners to theological insight and ethical transformation by proposing this novel metaphor of God's universal and impartial love. And his words speak with resonance, with *hibiki*.

Nor is this an isolated instance. Jesus also speaks of sparrows sold for a farthing, of lilies of the fields, of trees that bear good fruit and others that are barren, and in all of these instances he finds rich metaphors for the quality of God's care of persons. Further, he describes his own manner of life in terms of images drawn from nature.

> Foxes have holes, and birds of the air have nests;
> but the Son of man has nowhere to lay his head. [Matt. 8:20]

Here perhaps we touch upon the most remarkable fact of all. The Jesus of the sayings is an essentially homeless person, who is at home in all of the natural environment. In the *Poetics of Space,* Gaston Bachelard remarks on the importance of houses in the forming of human sensibility of space: "Our house is our corner of the world. . . . It is our first universe, a real cosmos in every sense of the word. . . . Memories of the outside world will never have the same tonality as those of home."[6] Yet it seems that Jesus' spatial sensibility is informed not so much by houses as by his experience of the natural environment. For him the outdoors is never hostile, but is rather the place of God's presence.

Recall that Jesus was born, according to the tradition, in a borrowed stable, and that his final act with the disciples, the last supper, occurred in another borrowed room. While Jesus is often a guest in the houses of others, it seems he has no house of his own. Eduard Schillebeeckx has pointed to the importance of the table fellowship in the ministry of Jesus. Meals with Jesus have a central place in the Gospel narratives. But note that most often Jesus is the guest at meals in the houses of others. One of the central occasions at which Jesus is the host is the feeding of the five thousand. This occurs in an outdoor space chosen by Jesus. It is a kind of picnic! The last supper forms a kind of link between this meal and that on the beach to which Jesus invites his disciples after the crucifixion (John 21:4-14.). Jesus is at home at the feasts of others, just as he is at home in the variety of outdoor meals he hosts.

Jesus leads the life of an itinerant preacher, evidences no craving to settle down and find "a place of his own." At times, to be sure, Jesus seeks solitude. On these occasions he goes to a lonely place on some hillside or garden, so that he can commune with the Father. He needs no temple, no room of his own, to commune with God. Indeed, rather the contrary: he seeks his communion with God in the homing environment of the outdoors. Likewise he is tempted in the outdoors, in the dwelling of the prophets, the wilderness.

Jesus needs no special home of his own, for he is at home in nature; his own place is the Palestinian countryside.

We should not get the impression that Jesus is alienated from the cities and villages of his homeland. These too he enters and finds in them natural acquaintance with their inhabitants. Jesus is not an agrarian in the sense of one who rejects progress and the life of the city. His life freely engages with the social realities of urban life. Yet it is notable how often he seems to stand *outside* cities. It is from a vantage point outside the city that he weeps over Jerusalem. His weeping over the cities of Chorazin, Bethsaida, and Capernaum also places him, physically and psychologically, outside the cities. One of the striking city images from the sayings of Jesus relates to a city set upon a hill which cannot be hidden. Apt as this image is to make the point that light cannot be hidden, we notice that it too is an image of one standing outside a city and seeing it from a hill or a dark roadside.

It would be possible to overstate this point, to suggest that Jesus is some kind of pioneer outdoorsman. Such is not the intention. Rather, it is to suggest that Jesus lives in a relationship of intimacy with both the natural and the constructed environment, and that he draws upon images of the natural environment with remarkable frequency and freedom. Here he continually finds parables of God's presence and God's loving care. It is not that Jesus personalizes nature, as we might put it; rather, it is that for Jesus the environment is the living symbol of God's presence. And since all things are ordered according to God's will and purpose, it is only to be expected that Jesus' eye should find in natural images the resonances that point to the love and glory of the Father.

Jesus, then, lives his life "in place." Not for him the placelessness of our modern experience. Jesus is at home in the environment and can reflect deeply the presence and the resonance of the environment in his parables and aphorisms, in his dialogues and stories. It is something of this quality of a life "in place" that we see at the root of the solution to our environmental crisis and that we seek to recover for contemporary consciousness.

2. THE CHRISTIFICATION OF HOLY SPACE

In our understanding of Jesus Christ we cannot remain with the historical Jesus. Although it is clearly the place to begin, we cannot stay with who Jesus *was*; we must move on to consider the broader christological question of who Jesus *is*. In making this move, however, we must not lose sight of the Jesus we have glimpsed in the recorded sayings. Indeed, we must look to the ministry of Jesus of Nazareth to test the various understandings of the Christ. This will especially be true as we seek to relate the Incarnation to the land.

The christification of holy space points to the process whereby the holiness of the places of Judaism were replaced with the holiness of a person in early Christianity. In earlier chapters we have indicated the second part of this process, in which the places of Jesus' earthly life themselves became sanctified through the memory of his presence. If we have established the evidence for the first part of this process, it is now time to attend to the second part. The transformation of the places of Jesus' life is evidenced in the formation of the Gospel narratives and their placement at the head of the New Testament canon.

The emergence of the Gospels witnesses a concern for the concrete details of the life and ministry of Jesus Christ. These details include a concern for geography together with a concern for history. The physical reality of the Christ event is being documented, and that physical reality is both temporal and spatial. Especially in this postresurrection period the danger existed that the experience of a transcendent Christ might engulf the memory of the earthly Jesus. Thus we see the Gospel writers recording the places in which Jesus lived, ministered, and died with careful attention to detail. It was important to them to record the fact that Jesus was actually present at these earthly locations.

The historical and geographical concern of the Gospel

97

writers has a theological foundation. Central to the entire New Testament is the Christian claim that in Jesus Christ the Word became flesh. We must immediately set this claim in the context of the concreteness of Yahweh's dealings with Israel, for it is of a piece with them. It is in this event that the earliest Jewish Christians found the fulfillment of their expectation for the Messiah, for a new activity of Yahweh such as prophetic faith had taught them. Davies points to the significance of this teaching in the consideration of the concrete elements of Jewish faith: Jerusalem, the temple, the land: "The Doctrine that the Word became flesh, although it resulted in a critique of distinct, traditional, holy places, demanded the recognition that where the Glory had appeared among men all physical forms became suffused with it."[7] The Word of God, incarnate in Jesus Christ, has a transformative effect on the places he encountered.

Generations of Christians since the Gospel writers have found a similar fascination with the places of Jesus' life. Without necessarily wishing to make them shrines, these persons testify to the importance of the concrete earthiness of the memory of Jesus. Their fascination with travel to the Holy Land testifies to a hidden relevance of these places to the lives they must live in other places, lives they seek to live "in Christ." Neither the resurrection of Jesus nor the sending of the Holy Spirit has diminished for them the spiritual importance of the place and the time of Jesus' short life, just as it was for the Gospel writers. The historical Jesus must be understood as the flesh of Palestine.

Here, then, is the immediate outworking of the christification of holy space. This theme can be further articulated by attention to the message of the kingdom of God in Jesus' preaching and in his work of gathering together a community. It is now widely acknowledged that the kingdom of God forms the centerpiece of Jesus' entire preaching. If that kingdom is not to be identified politically with the land of Israel, it nevertheless becomes the bearer of all the hopes and expectations that the Jews located in the promised land. The kingdom is the fulfillment of all the promises of God.

One of the persistent questions of New Testament scholarship has been, When does the kingdom of God arrive? The answer given by the acts of Jesus seems to be, "Now, in the very act of this proclamation of mine." In Jesus' ministry the kingdom is not identified as some distant future event so much as a reality whose presence is already breaking into human history. Still, his words point also to a future time, "when I will return." Both aspects must be held in tension in any interpretation of the time of the kingdom.

The present aspect of the presence of the kingdom is aptly expressed by Jesus' practice of table fellowship with sinners. In this fellowship Jesus welcomes all manner of persons into the kingdom as a present reality. They celebrate the joy and freedom of this presence. In this phase Jesus' ministry makes people glad. Jesus does not call for fasting, for repentance, in preparation for a future coming kingdom; rather, he invites persons to join with him in celebrating the presence of God in this very event, whether of proclamation or of fellowship. It is a truly remarkable feature of Jesus' public ministry that tax collectors, prostitutes, Pharisees, and Gentiles—both men and women—are invited to enjoy table fellowship with Jesus. Here the messianic expectation of plenty is enacted and fulfilled. It is little wonder that later Christian reflection saw the messianic banquet actually occurring, the kingdom actually dawning in the ministry of Jesus.[8]

The dawning of the kingdom with the ministry of Jesus and the climactic events of the crucifixion and resurrection did not, however, exhaust the expectation of the kingdom. A future component is still present. This was already noted in the sayings of Jesus. "Thy kingdom come," the disciples were instructed to pray. "If I go I will come again" is an especially significant saying of Jesus recorded in the Gospel of John at the end of his ministry.

The expectation of a future *parousia* plays such a significant role in the formation of the faith of the early

Christian community that it cannot be dismissed as having no rootage in the actual preaching of Jesus. Yet precisely what form that *parousia* would take is a subject for interpretation within the very pages of the New Testament. Thus it is clear that for Paul the end-time was imminent, and that for him life in the present must be lived in the tension of the "not yet." For Luke, on the other hand, the presence of the Spirit in the life of the early church constituted some kind of fulfillment of the expectation for Jesus' return. For Luke the kingdom is coming in the spread of the Christian gospel throughout the width and breadth of the Roman Empire. These differing interpretations point to the fact that the future reference of the kingdom of God was strongly present in the early Christian community. It is clear, however, that this future reference did not obscure the present experience of the kingdom.

The question about the kingdom's location also has a spatial dimension. In our enthusiasm for the question "When?" we must not lose the importance of asking about the location of the kingdom, its place in the vast reaches of space. The answer is not difficult to find. If the kingdom of God dawned in the very acts of Jesus, then the kingdom is identified with the presence of Jesus. Just as the kingdom dawns in the event of Jesus Christ, so the kingdom is present where Jesus is present. Here we begin to find the answer to the question concerning the "where" of the kingdom.

The question of the location of the kingdom is further clarified by attention to the gathering of a community, which was a central element of Jesus' earthly ministry. In eschewing a political role Jesus turned to fashioning a community that would turn the people of Israel into a true people of God. In gathering his disciples and sending them out on mission Jesus did not seek some sort of political overthrow, but rather the continuation of his own ministry and work of proclamation. Schillebeeckx remarks, "Jesus did appoint disciples as his co-workers and send them out to proclaim . . . the message of the coming rule of God, as well as to heal the sick and drive out devils."[9] The ministry of

100

Jesus' disciples led to the gathering of a community around the expectation of the kingdom of God.

Davies writes that the aim of Jesus "focused on the creation of a community worthy of the name of the people of God within Israel."[10] This community was to be loving, serving, and ultimately inclusive. Whereas the Pharisee Hillel sought to build a community centered on the Torah and the land, Jesus sought a universal, loving community in which the narrow political expectation of the restoration of the land to Israel played a minor part. Jesus' vision of the kingdom of God was broader and deeper than the view of the Zealots.

From the ministry of Jesus, then, we learn that the kingdom of God was present in his proclamation and table fellowship. This also points to the spatial presence of the kingdom of God, which was to be celebrated and enjoyed by all people in the presence of Jesus. Yet just as the kingdom had a present and a future reference, so the location of the kingdom had both an immediate and a more distant location. Just as the kingdom is exclusively related to the presence of Jesus Christ in both its present and its future modalities, so in its spatial implications the kingdom was to center in the very flesh of Jesus. So long as Jesus was bodily present with his disciples, they were not to fast. But once Jesus was taken away, then was the time to fast and to reflect upon both the futurity of the kingdom and its more distant spatial implications. The futurity of the kingdom was associated with the return of Jesus, and this must also have provided the immediate answer to the question of the ultimate location of the kingdom. But where was the kingdom to be located in the period between Jesus' death and Jesus' return, after he was no longer with the disciples in the flesh and before his coming in glory?

Here it is important to reflect on the experience of the post-Easter community of Christians. The Easter experience was for them no less than the experience of the continuing presence of Jesus. For these Christians the resurrection meant that Jesus Christ could never be taken away from them. His words, "Where two or three are gathered in my name, there am I in the midst of them" (Matt. 18:20) had now reached fulfillment. In the power of the Holy Spirit, given at Pentecost, the now ascended Jesus Christ is present with them in all the places of their lives. Thus, while continuing to hope in a future manifestation of the kingdom, the post-Easter Christians came to understand that the blessings of the kingdom were theirs already, in anticipation, in their present experience of the risen Christ. The power of the Holy Spirit was the experiential guarantee of the resurrection of Jesus and his presence in their midst. That presence signified for them the reality of the kingdom in their midst, even as they awaited for its final manifestation at the *parousia*.

In answer to the question of the locality of the kingdom of God there must be a tension. If the postresurrection location of the kingdom is where two or three are gathered in Jesus' name, then we have the tension between each particular location and the sum total of all such locations. It is in this sense that we should think of the kingdom as universal. It is not so much that the cosmic Christ is present universally, for stated in that way the meaning of Christ's presence undergoes a nonbiblical dilution and trivilization. Rather, the Spirit of the risen Christ is present wherever communities gather in Jesus' name.

In other words, the kingdom of God has both a primary local meaning and a secondary universal meaning. Each is needed in the life of Christian communities. The assurance that Jesus Christ is here, that God chooses to dwell with this community in this place, is the basis for a local incarnational life style. But equally the knowledge that God's kingdom is ultimately inclusive of all localities gives us a healthy reminder that our local life style must mesh with the needs of other localities. The environmental implications of this tension, or dialectic, are profound. The subtle interrelationship of the "macro" and the "micro" is the only way to offer a manageable and responsible program of environmental care.

What are the implications of this for our theme of the land? The presence of God's kingdom can mean no less than that the blessings of the promised land find their fulfillment in Jesus Christ. This is the position to which the New Testament gives emphasis: that all the blessings associated with the land—security, peace, and plenty in the presence of God—are now directly connected with the presence of Jesus Christ. In other words, in Jesus Christ all the promises of God come to their fulfillment. It is this understanding that the New Testament judges to be in accord with the ministry of the earthly Jesus. For the earthly Jesus comes to proclaim the kingdom of God, and that kingdom supersedes all earthly kingdoms in that it establishes the rule of God.

All the expectation for holy space, for the blessings of the land, are concentrated in Jesus Christ. The christification of holy space does not in any way spiritualize or dilute the concrete focus of Israel's hopes. On the contrary, it provides them with an even more concrete locus, namely the body of Christ, understood first in terms of the earthly presence of Jesus but second as the designation for the Christian community.

This is the proper fulfillment of the promises of the land. No longer can the community of faith hope for God to give them a special land, exclusively for their use. No longer can they expect that God will unite all God's blessings of peace, security, and plenty in one physical locality. For God has concretely located those in the person and work of Jesus Christ. The resurrection of Jesus Christ and his ongoing presence in the life of the Christian community transforms the old promise without destroying or spiritualizing it. By dwelling with the human community in and through Jesus Christ, God has demonstrated that God wills to dwell in the environment of each community. Further, God has entrusted to those redeemed by Christ the task of fashioning the dwelling place of God. That this should involve at least loving care of the environment is obvious. That it should encompass the work of justice and peace, the building of security and plenty for the human community on an inclusive

103

and universal scale, follows directly from the table ministry of Jesus.

If the place of God's presence is in the Christian community, this insight has implications for our understanding of the spatial implications of the Incarnation. It suggests that the Incarnation must be understood in terms of an ongoing process. The Incarnation tells us that God has taken up dwelling with humanity in the event of Jesus Christ. While the focus of debate has usually been upon what this doctrine claims about the person of Jesus Christ, it is important to think of its implication in the post-Easter period. In this period of gospel history—for example, in Acts and in the thinking of Paul—the notion of God dwelling with humanity is not retracted. Rather, it is extended in the emphasis upon the presence of the Holy Spirit within the community of believers. The Holy Spirit at times is understood as the presence of the risen Christ and at other times as the direct presence of God. But however the Spirit is understood, God is now understood to dwell with the Christian community.

Their task then became to realize in their actions the truth that this is where God wills to dwell. This meant loving and caring for the place as God cares for all the creatures of nature in Jesus' parables and sayings. It means not only to love and do justice but also to preserve and make fruitful the land, to fashion an environment in which the love of God may be shown forth by fashioning the environment for God's own dwelling. For the message of the Incarnation is that the dwelling of God is with the human community. The community's task is then to carry through the Incarnation of God into the places and times of their scattered lives.

Here we may make a connection with Jesus' being at home in the natural environment and living in intimacy with his surroundings. If Jesus was at home in the places of his life, it was because he knew that God was dwelling with him, extending his kingdom to these places. These places, in turn, became to Jesus the occasion of metaphors of God's loving presence and the moral truth which God established. In like manner, then, the Christian communities were to find their place in the localities in which God had established them. If in his life Jesus sanctified places by his presence and loving relationship, so too the community was to sanctify and care for the places of their life. If God was really present where the name of Jesus was spoken, if the Spirit mediated the presence of the risen Christ to all Christ's people, then the Incarnation was an ongoing process that needed to be a central element of the understanding and practice of the Christian communities.

The christification of holy space does not end with the ministry of the historical Jesus. The task of the community is to realize the presence of Christ in their midst, to become the surrogates for Jesus' presence. This has the spatial implication that they must seek to sanctify the places of their life in the name of Jesus. According to this extension of the Incarnation, in the localities of their lives God is present.

3. INCARNATION AS THE FOUNDATION OF A THEOLOGY OF THE LAND

If the Incarnation of God in Jesus Christ marks the concretion of all the hopes for a land of peace, security, and plenty, and the reality of the human community in Christ constitutes the dwelling of God with humanity, what does the Incarnation have to say to our concept of space? How does the notion of incarnation accord with or modify the received notions of space? It is clear that in the history of the concept of space a variety of notions emerged and that not all of them were congenial to the concept of incarnation.

First, if space is understood as a finite container, then the Incarnation represents God's entry into finite space. Yet how can the infinite God be contained in such a limited container? *Finitum non capax infiniti:* the finite cannot contain the infinite. Precisely this issue is the struggle of Thomas Aquinas and Martin Luther in their various christologies. By seeing space as "container," this view inevitably raises the question of containing God. We are driven deep into paradox. God's entry into space and time involves an apparent disregard for or overthrow of the natural orders of space and time. There is no way, according to this view, in which the Incarnation can be seen to uphold and enhance the natural orders of reality.

Second, if God is understood as the infinite receptacle, then it is space and time which find their place in God. In the frame of Newton's thought, then, God is the ultimate container of all things, including the man Jesus Christ. *Infinitium capax finiti:* the infinite contains the finite. But how can there be an incarnation? Can the infinite container of all things become one of the things it contains? Could God become a part of God without ceasing to be God? These difficulties stand in the way of a clear formulation of the Incarnation in this way of thinking.

Third, if space is understood as an expression of the rationality of God, then certainly there is no difficulty for God to be united with space. But in this view God is limited to this creation; its space is the expression of God's rationality and God is not free to exhibit any other rationality, any other pattern of being. This line of necessity also rules out incarnation as a free decision of God to enter into deepest unity with one person at one place and time. Rather, all of the creation within space and time is already expressive of God's rationality. All things *are* the Incarnation in space and time of God. This type of panpsychism or nonincarnationism has gained some popularity in the modern period. It claims to accept an Einsteinian view of space, and in a way not dissimilar to Newton understands this space as the "body" of God.[11] The problem with this view is that it dissolves the particularity of Christ's body into the immensity of God's body. By so doing, it not only contravenes a central New Testament emphasis, but in its dissolution of the miracle of the Incarnation it accedes in the modern dissolution of place into space. In the New Testament, Jesus Christ is the one chosen of God for God's

106

entry into space and time. By taking away the miracle of the Incarnation, this view reduces incarnation to a general principle of physical reality.

There is another way, which has been outlined by Thomas Torrance. Torrance begins by accepting the Einsteinian view of space as the seat of relations. This view, he holds, is not dissimilar to one held by some of the early Greek Fathers of the Christian Church. Here the distinction between God and the world is maintained by means of the notion of creation, so that space and time are conceived as created forms of rationality which exhibit ordered patterns of relationship that are still distinguishable from the eternal rationality of God. This is a world similar to the world of space/time relations envisaged in the Einsteinian view of space. Further, since the rationality of space is not identified with the eternal rationality of God, it makes sense to speak in terms of God entering time and space, and becoming one with created reality. God, acting out of freedom and not necessity, enters fully into that which God is not. It is not necessary to say that the rationality of space and time opposes the rationality of God. Rather, in coming into relation with God in this way, created space and time find their fulfillment in relation to God's eternal order and purpose.

It is on the basis of this fourth possibility that Torrance builds his case that the Incarnation in space and time established a set of real relations between God and the space and time of our earthly habitation. In other words, the Incarnation "asserts the reality of space and time for God in the actuality of His relations with us, and at the same time binds us to space and time in all our relations with Him."[12] If space and time are real for God in the Incarnation, they are no less real for us in our attempts at obedient discipleship. The Christian life, in other words, is rooted deeply in the orders of space and time.

By the concrete reality of God's relation with human communities, space and time are confirmed as the real location of their lives. Such communities do not have their real life in some extraspatial or eternal spiritual realm. They live in real space and time, and that means in all the ambiguities, risks, and challenges of actual history in actual geography. Simply by being related to this God who is identified by the Incarnation in Jesus Christ, such communities are placed and located in time. They become the agents, in Brueggemann's words, of "placed history." They cannot avoid their contract with space and time. Torrance remarks, "We can no more contract out of space and time than we can contract out of the creature-Creator relationship."[13]

This understanding of the Incarnation argues piowerfully against the spiritualizing tendench we have discussed in relation to Christian understandings of the land and space. The metaphor of ascent, which Santmire finds at the heart of the Christian tradition, is brought into a radical critique by this view of the Incarnation. In the Incarnation, God declares for all humankind to see that God's way with humanity lies in space and time and not in the rarefied heights of spiritual transport. This has importance for both a theology of the land and an understanding of the imperatives of Christian discipleship.

Further, this understanding of the Incarnation offers a way to define place. If mathematical space dissolves place, incarnation in mathematical space reconstitutes place. In this light, place is the location in time and space in which God becomes incarnate. In Chrisian history this has a determinate, specific meaning. In the person of Jesus Christ, in the history of the first century and the geography of ancient Palestine, God chose to become human. In the life of the communities which draw their identity from Jesus Christ, this becoming human in space and time continues. God chooses to dwell in the places of these human communities, and this has historical and geographical significance. It means that in their lives distinct places are constituted within the "trackless wilderness" of contemporary space and time.

The event of Jesus Christ thus reestablishes the reality of "place." By defining the locus of God's encounter with humanity, not in a generalized view of universal space but in a particular place, the Incarnation reconstitutes place as a concept for human living and self-understanding.

> This relation established between God and man in Jesus Christ constitutes Him as *the place* in all space and time where God meets with man in the actualities of human existence, and man meets God and knows Him in His own divine Being. . . . Jesus Christ [is] God's place in this world where He is present in our place. . . . It is not some ideal world but in our estranged world that God does this. It is place in which God has condescended to enter within the spatial context in order to bring His boundless Being to bear directly on man, so that we must think of that real presence not apart from the objective determinations and conditions of our physical existence.[14]

The place of the encounter with God is the place of our communal habitation. When Jesus speaks of the two or three gathered in his name, he speaks not only of the reality of his presence. He indicates a new understanding of the human location. For postmodern Christians he speaks of the reconstitution of the places of their lives. In this way the sense of place, so widely eulogized and lamented, is resurrected. The encounter which God has chosen binds our humanity to the places and times of our earthly lives.

In the calling of Israel and the gift of a land, and later in the calling of the church and the gift of a Son, God has chosen to encounter human persons in the concrete circumstances of their lives. If the encounter with God has personal and communal transformation as its goal and telos, that transformation must be understood in ethical and temporal terms. It is an encounter that embraces all of life—our work, the food we eat, and places we choose to inhabit, and the relationships with the earth we choose to enter to sustain our lives. It is at this point that the strong implications of the incarnational view of God's relation to space and time begin to emerge.

The implication of the reconstitution of place in the life of the human community is that it in its turn must love and care for the place as the very dwelling place of God. The discovery and elaboration of what this means can be project of learning and discipleship for the community. At the very least, the dwelling place of God should include making it habitable for all of God's creatures, so that birds of the air and fish of the water may once again share habitation with human communities. Beyond that, the rendering beautiful the places of our lives can assume a priority our technological mind set disallows. A reawakened sense of beauty of local places may fuel a deeply spiritual concern for the preservation of the ecological diversity and uniqueness of each place.

A central argument of this book has been that our ecological carelessness and profligacy have been fueled by the loss of the sense of place. Living in "placeless horizons of reach," we no longer distinguish one place from another except in terms of what access it provides on our toplogy of reach. We have suggested that this flagrant disregard for the uniqueness and beauty of particular places feeds into the exploitative attitudes our society so richly exemplifies. It is against all of this that we set the event of Jesus Christ as that which may be the turning point in the journey of human thought and spirituality.

If the Incarnation reconstitutes place for those communities shaped by the event of Jesus Christ, then it is the central item in a theology of the environment. Growing out of this doctrine may come a renewed sense of local discipleship, a new order of faithfulness that measures itself by nothing less than the fashioning of the dwelling place of God and all God's creatures. From this may flow a great reward of satisfaction and happiness. Through the Incarnation in Jesus Christ we may discover again sustaining and sustainable space, the contours of what Bachelard calls "felicitous space." How this may be expressed in practice in communities of the place-constituting Incarnation is the subject of chapter 6.

CHAPTER SIX

Defining Incarnational Praxis

Up to this point several specifications of the sense of place have been advanced. The sense of place is a fundamental aspect of human being and of human religion, as is borne out by the analysis of its role in Aboriginal religion and the Hebrew Scriptures. Yet it has been threatened by the development of the Western philosophical tradition and thrown into jeopardy by the transition from the holy places of Judaism to the universal reach of Christianity. The shattering of Judaism's territorial chrysalis, however, opened the way for the discovery that God could be worshiped in the many places God's people found themselves.

In turn the Incarnation declared and demonstrated that God's dwelling is in the person of Jesus Christ, who continues to live in the places and times of the human community. This implication of the Incarnation is actualized in the dwelling of God's Spirit with the communities of faith scattered throughout the world. The indwelling of the Holy Spirit not only creates community anew but brings the presence of God into experiential reality. The places of the human community are created anew, rendered holy by the transforming presence of the triune God. The reconstitution of place is seen as the practical implication of the Incarnation.

But how can this understanding of the Incarnation be carried into practice? What are the down-to-earth steps whereby the places of our lives can be reconstituted? To answer this question one final specification of the sense of place must be added, that which emerges in the art of our culture. By turning to some of the living poetry of our day, we may begin to address the issue of an environmental praxis for our place and time. A discussion of the full range of such poetry lies beyond the scope of this work, and we must be content to sample and highlight rather than to exhaust the subject. The specification of the sense of place through poetry will point up the final connection be made, that between the experience of place in our culture and the "dreaming" of our people.

1. POETRY AND THE SENSE OF PLACE

The rootage of aesthetic sensibility in a sense of place is evidenced widely in our literature. So intimate is the connection between the work of some poets and the places they inhabit that it seems a gross oversimplification of the relation to say simply that their poetry is descriptive of the place or that it is expressive of the poet's feelings in relation to the place. We are drawn again to the insight of Gaston Bachelard which suggests that in the poetic image places themselves find voice. The poet becomes the medium for the place itself.

Such a view obviously presupposes a different way of seeing and thinking about the environment. No longer simply a backdrop for human activity, it becomes itself a subject of certain activities and possesses rights of its own. As such, it is more than simply a resource for human exploitation and becomes part of the web of life in which human life is bound with other life by bonds of mutual dependency. Attention to the work of our poets provides us a beginning in the new ways of thinking and seeing that are foundational to the fashioning of a new environmental praxis.

112

DEFINING INCARNATIONAL PRAXIS

A North American poet who has sung the song of a threatened land is the man who has written most searchingly of the issues of agriculture and the land, Wendell Berry. This poem is simply titled "1979 VIII" in his recent collection called *Sabbaths*:

> I go from the woods into the cleared field:
> A place no human made, a place unmade
> By human greed, and to be made again.
> Where centuries of leaves once built by dying
> A deathless potency of light and stone
> And mold of all that grew and fell, the timeless
> Fell into time. The earth fled with the rain,
> The growth of fifty thousand years undone
> In a few careless seasons, stripped to rock
> And clay—a "new land," truly, that no race
> Was ever native to, but hungry mice
> And sparrows and the circling hawks, dry thorns
> And thistles sent by generosity
> Of new beginning. No Eden, this was
> A garden once, a good and perfect gift;
> Its possible abundance stood in it
> As it then stood. But now what it might be
> Must be foreseen, darkly, through many lives—
> Thousands of years to make it what it was,
> Beginning now, in our few troubled days.[1]

The speaker is drawn to a place he knows very well, a cleared field adjacent the woods where he has often found sabbath in meditation. The field no less than the woods is a place, a place not made by humans but, paradoxically, unmade by human greed. In knowing this place the speaker also knows something of its history and finds there the challenge to a new remaking that will reflect more closely the richness and complexity, the freedom and perfection, of its original creation.

In our rush to exploit the environment we pit ourselves against the Creator, and places, unique in their nature and history, are destroyed. Another voice which celebrates the

113

images of locality, the spirit of places, is that of Judith Wright. Her poem "At Cooloola" tells of an Australian place:

The blue crane fishing in Cooloola's twilight
has fished there longer than our centuries.
He is the certain heir of lake and evening,
and he will wear their colour till he dies,

but I'm a stranger, come of a conquering people.
I cannot share his calm, who watch his lake,
being unloved by all my eyes delight in,
and made uneasy, for an old murder's sake.

Those dark-skinned people who once named Cooloola
knew that no land is lost or won by wars,
for earth is spirit: the invader's feet will tangle
in nets there and his blood be thinned by fears.

Riding at noon and ninety years ago,
my grandfather was beckoned by a ghost—
a black accoutred warrior armed for fighting,
who sank into bare plain, as now into time past.

White shores of sand, plumed reed and paperbark,
clear heavenly levels frequented by crane and swan—
I know that we are justified only by love,
but oppressed by arrogant guilt, have room for none.

And walking on clean sand among the prints
of bird and animal, I am challenged by a driftwood spear
thrust from the water; and, like my grandfather,
must quiet a heart accused by its own fear.[2]

A scene of natural tranquility opens before us, a crane fishing in a lake at twilight, a scene suggesting the quiet order of natural things. There is the suggestion of timelessness about this scene; for centuries it has been going on in precisely this way, for centuries "longer than our centuries." With this note Wright has introduced the central contrast of the poem, their time and ours. Though the speaker enjoys the place, though her eyes delight in what she sees, she is uneasy, burdened with the memory of an old murder. The Aborigines who named the lake Cooloola have a legitimacy of habitation like the crane's. It stretches beyond mere naming the place to understanding the earth and participation in the spirituality of the earth. This formed a bond deeper and truer than any conquering people can know, which suggests a curse upon those who come and try to wrest the land away from its rightful inhabitants: "the invader's feet will tangle / in nets there and his blood be thinned by fears." As if to shake off the shackles of that past with its strange tales, the speaker turns to the vivid beauty of the present. But turning her eyes back to the ground, the "clean sand," she is suddenly challenged by a driftwood spear. Now the guilt finds a definite occasion. The heart reverts to fear, and the attempt to move beyond the ghostly presence of the grandfather is circumvented. There is no escape.

Central in this poem is the theme of spiritual bonding to a place, the inner struggle to find in this place a home, a spiritual domicile. The speaker is doomed to fail in this struggle, though her eyes delight in all she sees, though the closeness of her observation and the discipline of her attention indicate her desire and willingness for a relation to the place and the depth of her identification with it. As she walks on the clean sand among the prints of birds and animals, she finds not comfort but challenge, not home but threat.

Of the Aborigines who once lived here, of the animals who presently inhabit the place, this observer, burdened with her knowledge and her guilt, must say, "They were here by right. They were here first. They belonged." Their spiritual bondedness to the land, which legitimated their possession of the land, throws into the question the claim of the conquering people, who came as invaders and murderers. Though the speaker deeply identifies with this place and exults in its beauty, she feels rejected by it. For her there is no justification, no love, only the need to "quiet a heart accused by its own fear."

A later poem, "Australia 1970," speaks in chilling apocalyptic tones, suggestive of a doomed world.

> Die, wild country, like the eaglehawk,
> dangerous till the last breath's gone,
> clawing and striking. Die
> cursing your captor through a raging eye.
>
> Die like the tigersnake
> that hisses such pure hatred from its pain
> as fills the killer's dreams
> with fear like suicide's invading stain.
>
> Suffer, wild country, like the ironwood
> that gaps the dozer-blade.
> I see your living soil ebb with the tree
> to naked poverty.
>
> Die like the soldier-ant
> mindless and faithful to your million years.
> Though we corrupt you with our torturing mind,
> stay obstinate, stay blind.
>
> For we are conquerors and self-poisoners
> more than scorpion or snake
> and dying of the venoms that we make
> even while you die of us.
>
> I praise the scoring drought, the flying dust,
> the drying creek, the furious animal,
> that they oppose us still;
> that we are ruined by the thing we kill.[3]

Here too we find images of resistance, a resistance of the land to the will of the conquerors. It is a resistance that becomes heroic in the light of the destruction that modern society has wrought. In some ways this poem could have been written in no other land than Australia. Its images speak of unique elements of the experience of the Australian landscape and the Australian creatures. Wright finds much to praise in the ability of this land to resist the designs of humanity. Perhaps few North Americans can identify with this voice. Wright has been in many ways an ecological prophet before her time. For decades now she has been sounding the alarm for our endangered environment. Yet little has been done. Wright's bitter experience has dimmed her hopes in the human community's ability to change its ways.

If Wright speaks with a pessimism born of her experiences, we should not brush her words aside as those of a doomsayer. Her poetry speaks out of the realism with which the ecological issue must be faced. In particular North Americans, nurtured in a rich and plenteous land and in traditions there were often grounded in easy optimism, need to listen to such voices as Wright's, speaking out of another place, another sense of reality.

Finally, from the wisdom of the Australian Aborigine, Kath Walker speaks. In modern poetry she upholds the tradition of the Aboriginal Dreaming and addresses profoundly the issues of environmental degradation. The poem "Time Is Running Out" speaks in apocalyptic terms which echo those of Judith Wright:

> The miner rapes
> The heart of earth
> With his violent spade.
> Stealing, bottling her black blood
> For the sake of greedy trade.
> On his metal throne of destruction,
> He labours away with a will,
> Piling the mountainous minerals high
> With giant tool and iron drill.
>
> In his greedy lust for power,
> Be destroys old nature's will.
> For the sake of the filthy dollar,
> He dirties the nest he builds.
> Well he knows that violence
> Of his destructive kind
> Will be violently written
> Upon the sands of time.

But time is running out
And the time is close at hand,
For the Dreamtime folk are massing
To defend their timeless land.
Come gentle black man
Show your strength;
Time to take a stand.
Make the violent minor feel
Your violent
Love of land.[4]

The images of this poem speak of violence and of gentleness, of forced change and the resistance to change. In our rush to industrial standardization we have lost many of the stories and the songs of the lands we settled. Yet the massing of the Dreamtime folk to defend the land speaks powerfully of forces that cannot be dismissed by our forgetfulness and laws of the land that will return to haunt a careless generation.

Berry, Wright, and Walker have used poetry to tell of the places they love, which are also the places they see being devastated by the "advances" of modern industry. In poetry they are able to speak of what is unique to these places and to what is uniquely threatened. In different ways the poems celebrate the localities which are threatened and yet also loved. As we face an uncertain environmental future in Australia and North America, ecologists and environmentalists must seek the aid of the poets and the painters.

Yet how can the vision of the poets mesh with religious belief and practice? In seeking to integrate these insights with those coming from the Christian understanding of the Incarnation we turn once again to the example of Aboriginal religion. Here we will find the clue to the fusion of religious belief with ecological praxis by means of the aesthetic.

2. ABORIGINAL DREAMING AND THE RECONSTITUTION OF PLACE

In the religion of the Australian Aborigine the events of the Dreaming transformed the bare, empty expanse of the

Australian landscape into definable places within the range of mythic history. The meandering tracks of the Dreaming heroes traversed homogeneous space and created within it places of beauty and distinction. In this way places were constituted and made fit for life—plant, animal, and human. Today, where Aboriginal culture is still alive the songs of these places are sung, and in that singing the ongoing reality of the places is assured. In the renewal of these places the hope for human life and the life of other species is sustained. In this vision human life and the life of the places are bound up inextricably, so that the care for the one follows naturally from the care of the other.

The power of the Dreaming is kept alive in the songs and dances of the Aboriginal people. The "pilgrimages" of the tribes along the tracks of the ancient songlines sustain the places and renew the bonds of the human community with its places.[5] The Dreaming has profound ecological consequences. Expressing the wisdom and knowledge which the Aboriginal people have acquired over the long period of continuous inhabitation of the particular territories, the Dreaming defines tribal territories in a manner that is extremely sensitive to the capacity of the land forms to support the total life of the tribal group. By circumscribing how much territory a given tribal group can traverse and "own," the sacred song cycles of the Dreaming delimit areas of precise scale. In the rehearsal of the mythic cycles each local group is reminded of its range and of the impinging ranges of other groups. The Dreaming has then provided for the ecological health not only of the environment but also of the human inhabitants.

The Aborigines can teach us much about a sense of place and its accompanying praxis. Their life is centered in the dances and songs of the Dreaming, and it is this aesthetic element of their life which continually draws them back to their religious sense of the land. Through the retelling of the Dreaming stories, the singing of the Dreaming songs, they become one with the place they inhabit. The fusion of the human and the environment by means of the aesthetic has profound implications for economic praxis. It renders the sort of alliance between human society and the environment that Wendell Berry heralds as the prerequisite for proper practice in agriculture and human life in the land. Not only the paths they must follow in sacred travel, but the patterns of their hunting and gathering are determined by the content of the Dreaming stories, songs, and dances.

Here we see the integration of the religious and the economic, of the aesthetic and the practical. This vision has deep relevance for our society as we seek an adequate environmental praxis. We have separated these elements of life—the religious and economic, the aesthetic and the practical—and we have thus surrendered a holistic vision to one conceived in narrowly economic and technological terms. The key to the reintegration of religion and economics may lie in the recovery of the aesthetic. In the words of Wendell Berry, if the aesthetics are right, the economics will also be right, just as satisfaction of the proper economic criteria will lead to the satisfaction of aesthetic criteria.[6] This is not to suggest a narrowly aesthetic view. In our approach to land use and land policy a larger integrative effort is necessary in which economics, religion, and aesthetics are fused together. By elaboration of the concepts of beauty and harmony, by a return to the refinement of the landscape, aesthetics may offer the means whereby the fusion of visions can occur.[7]

The relationship between the Aboriginal people and the places they inhabit has important implications for our understanding of the Incarnation. In its intimacy and mutuality this relationship shows us how properly to inhabit the environment of our life—an essential element of an incarnational life style. In coming to inhabit their places in dance, story, and song, the Aborigines teach us that properly to inhabit a place we must come to a deep knowledge of it and be able to celebrate and reaffirm that knowledge in the symbolic forms of our lives. In this way they teach us how to take the places and times of our lives with the religious seriousness they deserve. The Aborigines offer a profound example of an incarnational ethic of land care. In other words, they may teach us how to take the places and times of our lives with the seriousness and care which the dwelling of God with the human community requires.

This is certainly not to suggest that the Aborigines are incarnational Christians at heart. Clearly they are not, and they live within the structures of their own religion. There are interesting reports of syncretism in present-day traditional Aboriginal communities indicating certain ways in which the Aborigines adapt their religious symbols to encompass elements of Christian faith.[8] Such adaptations, however, are carried on from the perspective of their distinctive religious understanding. For these people the land as a whole is sacred, and the particular territory of the local group is charged with religious significance, sacred energy, and life-giving power.

For Christians religious significance, energy, and power can be identified only with God. Our access to that significance, energy, and power is through the indwelling of the Spirit of Christ. For us the earth is not intrinsically sacred; rather, as God's creation and gift it becomes sacred by the decision of God to dwell in space and time. To be sure, it has a special quality, rather like an original holiness, which even the activities of human pollution have not destroyed. While it has not escaped the effects of the fall—like us, it suffers in bondage—its corruption is somehow less far-reaching than our own. Its profanity is secondary, being derived from our profanity. However, its original holiness is still accessible and is restored through the act of God the Spirit, the creator of human community and the agent of the ongoing act of the Incarnation. The dwelling of God's Spirit with us transforms our perceptions of our place and imbues it with sacred qualities. As disciples of the risen Christ we are called to discover Christ's presence in our midst and to know that in the places of our lives the transformative presence of Christ's Spirit is active. Space becomes charged with religious meaning only as we realize the stupendous truth of the Incarnation and its transforming power in our lives.

In our theology, which diverges in fundamental ways from the thinking of Aboriginal culture, we need at this time in our history to be instructed by their culture in the practice that is proper to our faith. As partners in respectful dialogue we may learn from the Aboriginal people, who, perhaps more than any other, are a people of the land.

There is a special historical significance abut this learning, this dialogue. In recent history we have witnessed massive dispossession of people from their lands. The story of this dispossession is now coming to expression in various literary and artistic forms. On movie screens, in drama, and in fiction we are now being reminded of dreadful histories which we would probably rather forget. The story enters our consciousness, try as we might to forget and ignore it. The horror of the events comprising this history may not be forgotten or passed over in silence. Whether we think of the Australian context or that of North America, we see a similar pattern. In North America the dispossession of the indigenous people occurred in a series of bloody battles once celebrated as part of America heroic heritage. Now we must look more critically at this piece of the national past. If it was this struggle which opened the frontier and made possible the development of the country's immense natural resources, it was also the event which established patterns of systemic injustice in the relation of European settlers to the indigenous people of the land. The struggle of many Indian tribes for repossession of tribal lands continues today, just as the political struggle for land rights for the Australian Aborigine continues in Australia.

There can be no question that a Christian community committed to understanding the land in incarnational terms, informed by the biblical notion of covenant, must stand in support of those movements which seek to bring equitable and just occupation of lands to dispossessed peoples. In facing the tough political struggles in support of such policies, in Australia, the United States, and Third World countries, we will need to draw deeply from the resources of faith and the longing for justice that the biblical tradition nurtures in us. Nor should we be dead to the insight that as dispossessors we shall never find peace in the land until justice for the dispossessed is done. It is profoundly fitting that we turn to the dispossessed to find wisdom in the face of the destruction we have wrought in these lands. Indeed, our chance of finding ecological health is dependent upon our learning the wisdom of the indigenous people in the terms of their land tenure.

3. GRASS-ROOTS PROJECTS FOR THE INCARNATIONAL CHURCH

If our whole lives are bound up with the land, and if our physical, spiritual, emotional, and communal life flows out of the relationship with the locality we inhabit, then issues of the locality need to become the focus of our corporate and religious life. This insight is in line with the implications of the Incarnation for our understanding of place. Further, it squares with the understanding of the church we have developed. As much as anything the churches may *do,* there is a far more significant ministry in what churches *are.* Their reality is to be the local expressions of the kingdom of God, and their calling is to incarnate in this locality the love and care with which God loves all of the creation.

If the task of the local church is to love the place with the love that God has for all creation, what does it mean to love a place? Here once again the ways of the Australian Aboriginal may direct us. To love a place is to seek its well-being and the well-being of the creatures it supports. Yet human society so often means the superposition of another concern entirely, namely, the exploitation of the wealth of a place. What we need to recapture is a sense of the well-being of the whole spectrum of life, from which human society cannot be isolated. Since our Western technological consciousness has drawn us away from this understanding, we must work very consciously and deliberately to recover what is axiomatic and unconscious in Aboriginal culture. Deliberate attention to what fits harmoniously with what is already present in the place and what enhances the beauty of the place enables us to move in the right direction. In these aesthetic terms we may begin to find once again the vision of the whole in which human society is fully integrated into the life of nature. In this way our communities may incarnate the love of God.

Within the incarnational church, then, the issues and problems of the locality will be the focus of intense concern and reflection. Local discipleship becomes the key concept. In particular, discipleship must embrace economics and the issues of proper livelihood.[9] By thinking locally we can act in ways that begin to affect the wider picture, for there is no global issue that is not first a local issue. The macro and the micro are intimately related. If we are able to think locally, we will see that by beginning small, with local issues, we can in our way contribute to the solution of global problems. Thus, we may not be able to reduce the ozone depletion of our upper atmosphere, but we can quit using aerosol cans with fluorocarbon propellants. Or we may not be able to do anything about the deforestation of the Amazon basin, but there is something we can do about the reforestation of our local community. Plant a tree! Local acts of care spark other acts and lead us naturally to think in terms of wider needs.

But how can this theological vision be brought into practice? In what follows, I outline a five-step plan to enable local congregations to set about the task of defining local discipleship in their place.

Step 1: A Contextual Analysis

Since we have not developed a tradition of local knowledge, such as is preserved in Aboriginal culture by the songs and stories of the Dreaming, we must set about to acquire such knowledge and to integrate it into a body of wisdom. An analysis of our context must be the first step in our procedure. Such an analysis must begin with the facts and figures that the sciences of demographics and economics provide. These means provide insight into the present situation, but we must also see that what is present grows out of the past. A history of the people and their enterprises in the place can round out our view of the place. Here knowledge and insight from all members of the community are invaluable. Unexpected sources of knowledge must be tapped, not only the economic and historical experts, but also the elderly whose cultural memory is keen. From this body of knowledge of the place may come a renewed sense of what activities are possible and desirable here. From our sense of the capabilities of the place may come a surer sense of its future possibilities.

In an attempt to follow my own counsel, let me reflect on my location in Dayton, Ohio. At United Theological Seminary we inhabit a beautiful 35-acre site. Each year in the spring we celebrate Arbor Day. The tradition of celebrating Arbor Day goes back to the work of Merl W. Harner, New Testament professor between 1927 and 1965, who planted thousands of trees on the campus, of which some 585 survived in 1985.[10] At my suggestion the name was changed in the late seventies to Earth Day, this term seeming to speak more to the spirit of our times. But whether as Arbor Day or Earth Day the purpose and function of the day is the same. It is devoted to the care of the trees on our property and to the planting of new trees, shrubs, and gardens. From this annual event a new sense of carrying on the tradition of the care of the earth and the love of this place emerges.

A contextual analysis should become a sustained agenda for each ministering community. Contextual analyses must not rest content with demographic facts and some brief history of the church. Demographics is important, as is analysis of the economy of the locality and the broader economic trends that are affecting life in the community. Insights from all members of the congregation and the local community must be sought in learning more about the issues and agendas of the community, with special attention being given to ecological factors.

The main task of the members of the church is to know these facts and to ask themselves continually, What do they express about the kingdom of God in this place? In other words, their task moves from demographics and economics to theological interpretation. They must seek to articulate the vision and perspective of the Christian tradition in their setting. If they do their theology well, and if it is built upon a solid fund of local knowledge, they will soon find themselves generating specific proposals for ways in which the church may embody Christ and serve the kingdom of God in this place.

Step 2: The Practice of Hospitality

A sense of hospitality is seen in the ministry of Jesus and in the practice of the Aborigines. In our culture we are conditioned to think in acquisitive and possessive terms: what is mine is mine and should remain so, just as what is yours is yours and should remain so. If we are to learn the new ways of incarnational discipleship, we must begin to move toward the sort of interdependence that hospitality suggests.

Belonging to a certain place is not the same as defending a piece of turf. In our suburban Dayton community attempts have been made to organize our community by establishing procedures to watch for criminal activity in the area. We have Neighborhood Watch groups that seek to monitor unrecognized vehicles coming into our blocks. This is an example of defending our turf. But what has brought a sense of belonging is the set of personal relationships facilitated by the Neighborhood Watch program. These relationships and this sense of belonging have enabled us to "inhabit" this neighborhood. From this base projects have multiplied. Working together on the beautification of our neighborhood, sharing in political campaigns, and focusing on things that we can do as a community have together effected a sense of local identity and belonging.

At times the dangers of gentrification and elitism emerge. "Upgrading" a neighborhood often comes to mean the exclusion of persons of lesser income or of another race. For Christian churches there is a challenge here. The neighborhood church can say that the God it worships chooses to dwell in this neighborhood, and that none of God's children can be excluded. In the light of this vision the task is not one of expanding one's own turf and excluding those of lesser income or social standing; rather the task is to offer the hospitality of God to those neighbors who share and those who desire to share this locality. We are reminded of Jesus' table fellowship and his practice of hospitality. How can we as churches and local communities practice a similar hospitality? It seems to me that we must come to think in terms not of defending the neighborhood from intrusion so much as welcoming into the neighborhood those who would choose to come, and then working with them in the particular needs and opportunities the neighborhood affords.

To be sure, the neighborhood has some rights to exclude some individuals and enterprises. But wealth and social class have little to do with this. Berry lists three questions that must be asked with respect to a human economy in any given place: What is here? What will nature permit us to do here? What will nature help us to do here?[11] A similar set of questions can shape the way in which a local community engages with new enterprises seeking to locate in their midst:

(1) What is here in terms of human resources, natural resources, existing facilties?

(2) What will the existing natural, human, and infrastructural resources permit us to do here?

(3) What will the existing community assist the new enterprise to accomplish here, and what will the new enterprise contribute to the life of the community?

By posing such a set of questions to incoming enterprises, communities can practice the kind of hospitality that is most profound, the welcoming of those who will be happy in this place and the exclusion of those who will be unhappy and who will bring unhappiness.

Step 3: Other Neighborhoods: Rural-Urban Linkages

Hospitality and interdependence are not only matters of one location, but find expression in the ways in which we relate to other neighborhoods. These may be expressed by the establishment of linkages of mutual assistance. It is very important to realize that the well-being of our neighborhood is bound up with the well-being of all other neighborhoods. The inhabitants of the secular city need to understand and to explore their commonality with the people of the land. To this end a pairing of the local church with another church in a different locality can be a means of extending fellowship and broadening Christian vision. If each urban parish were linked with a rural parish, several new opportunities would emerge. Visits, joint workshops, and retreats can become the occasions for the exploration of common concerns and of concerns specific to each location. More than anything else, entering into one another's lives and struggles can be a vital source of new energy and encouragement in the life of faith.

Linkage with a rural church can be the means whereby an urban church gains new awareness of the immediate problems of rural people and a broad understanding of the ecological issues we face. For a rural church linkage with an urban church can be a resource for further research and political strategizing. It is important that such relationships be established on the basis of mutuality and interdependence. The relationship cannot be set up as one of urban aid to rural communities in crisis, for such a pattern does not represent the reality and would induce atttitudes of patronage and dependency. Rather, as self-respecting communities churches can develop relationships based upon a common spiritual search and a common religious commitment. From such relationships further projects may spin off.

Step 4: Plant Trees and Gardens

Feeding our people in ways that are ecologically sound requires that we be very intentional about how we plant and how we harvest. The issues of food and of health are intimately linked, as are the health of the environment and human health. We all should seek a more active engagement in food production. The wartime practice of planting victory gardens could be revived by local communities. The Wegerzyen Gardens in Dayton makes available to urban dwellers a large field which is divided into small strips of land. Interested families are allotted a strip which they may garden to produce fresh produce in the summer months. There is no reason why other urban communities could not establish similar gardens on the outskirts of their cities. The gain in terms of produce is considerable, as is the sense of community that emerges in such projects.

Trees are the single most important element in the reviving of ecological health. A tree count of your neighborhood or farm is an important part of the contextual analysis. In rural areas tree planting can be coordinated in such a way as to reclaim desalinated areas or to form needed windbreaks. In suburban areas tree planting can be posed as an alternative to the growing of lawns. Lawns are costly in terms of the use of ground water and in terms of the amount of pointless labor involved in upkeep. The heavy use of chemicals that seems to go with lawn growing in North America is another strike against this practice, especially where ground water is already threatened with chemical pollution. Where water is scarce, this widespread practice does not make ecological good sense and should be discouraged. The growth of indigenous plants and grasses and their occasional mowing can lead to very attractive "front patches."

We should attempt to stop the paving of our land. In every city and town vast areas of cement and asphalt are now killing the soil. Parking lots, whose ugliness matches their ubiquity, offer no shade or protection and waste much good land. Could we not insist that our parking lots be fringed with gardens and trees? The establishment of local tree societies is one way to begin to have a voice in these matters.

The engagement of urban churches in gardening and tree planting projects can offer a practical way to enter into the crises of the land. By engaging in such tasks we begin, almost unconsciously, to undertake the broader tasks of keeping the gene pool diverse and monitoring the state of the soils and of the atmosphere. As we relearn to garden, we encounter all the problems of soil fertility, water supply, pest and weed control, and so on. A change in outlook can begin. Out of the real struggles and triumphs of the small gardener a new sense may emerge of the possibility of a sustainable agriculture in which the use of chemical and fossil fuel is minimized.

Teaching and instruction are very important in this connection. Here the work of such field research institutes as the Land Institute in Salina, Kansas, is very important in gaining knowledge about methods of sustainable agriculture.[12] Teaching and learning may be undertaken in conjunction with our rural partner church. The possibilities here for mutual instruction and dialogic learning are immense. I am convinced that farmers with a religious sense of the land are a great untapped resource in our search for ecological understanding. Not only can they teach us much about the tilling of the soil; they can demonstrate the deep sense of the earth and the love of the land.

The mystery of the incarnate God drives us to seek a deeper knowledge of the places we inhabit. Such knowledge grows out of story and song, and this suggests a final project.

Step 5: Collecting and Commissioning Local Art

The preservation of local knowledge and history can only occur as these are retold in story and image. What begins with the facts and figures of a contextual analysis must end with the incarnation of this knowledge in poem and song. If we are to learn what it means to dwell in a place, we will have to discover in it the songs and stories which speak of its uniqueness. For Australians part of this discovery will involve seeking out the stories and songs of the Aboriginal people. Christian churches should be in the forefront of the work of discovery. They should be teaching these stories and songs to their children, for only in such a way will the memories of a place be kept alive. New stories, songs, and poetry must also be encouraged and collected, so that we can

130

build up a body of work that reflects creatively on the place.

It is important that the question of an incarnational praxis be addressed in rather specific terms. This specificity must not be taken, however, as defining the limits of the possible. Quite the contrary. It is my conviction that attention to the specifics of each local situation is the way to push back the limits in our conception of what is possible. Specific instances will provide the stimulus to local churches to dream and then to implement projects that will reclaim the place in which they find themselves. Finally, however, we want to set the question of incarnational praxis in its proper and ultimate context.

4. THE WHOLE WORLD GROANS IN BONDAGE

The struggle to revive and preserve the localities we occupy will not be easy. Having done all we can, having utilized every possibility of group consciousness raising and political pressure, we may still find that we are wrestling with giants whose power far outstrips our own. In setting the theology of the land firmly in the context of the biblical struggle of a people for the promised land, we have identified a powerful resource to use in our struggle. We need not be surprised that we find ourselves in conflict with very powerful forces, for the biblical struggle for the promised land continues today in the struggle for economic justice and ecological sanity. Paul is under no illusions in this regard. We wrestle, he warns, against principalities, against powers, against the rulers of darkness of this world, against spiritual wickedness in high places (Eph. 6:12)

The notes of apocalypse and struggle have sounded in the poetry we have examined. Preservation of the gentle beauty of the places celebrated in the poetry calls for disciplined and sustained struggle. The apocalyptic strains in the poetry pick up on a well-established tradition in the Bible—the battle between the forces of good and evil, the struggle for the kingdom of righteousness and justice. In this context Paul remarks:

131

> For the creation waits with eager longing for the revealing of the sons of God; for the creation was subjected to futility, not of its own will but by the will of him who subjected it in hope; because the creation itself will be set free from its bondage to decay and obtain the glorious liberty of the children of God. We know that the whole creation has been groaning in travail together until now; and not only the creation, but we ourselves, who have the first fruits of the Spirit, groan inwardly as we wait for adoption as sons, the redemption of our bodies. (Rom. 8:19-23)

Paul sets the struggle between good and evil in a cosmic context. The struggle is for no less than the kingdom of God, and the power that is at work in us is no less than the power of God. In the language of apocalyptic we find the resource that enables us to be patient with an enduring hope in the midst of hardship. In the language of apocalyptic we point to the final aspect of incarnational praxis. In this apocalyptic framework we find the language of patience that endures and of hope in the midst of hardship.

We have seen how the language of apocalypticism was used during times of exile and dispossession to keep alive hope in the promises of Yahweh. And further, in the emerging Christian movement, these apocalyptic hopes and expectations came to focus in one person, Jesus Christ. For the early Christians all that they hoped for found its foundation in him. Our task, defined by this fact, is to keep this hope and expectation alive today. In God not one of our efforts is ever in vain. And there are things which no government department or powerful industry can take away from us. Foremost is the language of our hope and the stories of our Dreaming. Whenever we find ourselves up against situations in which it seems we can do little or nothing to change the destructive factors at work, we must realize the modesty of our enterprises and our role. Our main task, then and always, is to keep alive the language of faith, the songs of the Dreaming, the memory of Jesus Christ. If we can pass this language, these songs, this memory on to our children, we will have done a mighty thing. We will have sown the seeds of a better future. This is not to retreat into self-enclosed piety; but it is to acknowledge our own limitation and to find good work to do in the meantime, as we await the outworking of the powers of judgment.

In the wilderness the children of Israel experienced division between the older and the younger generations. The older ones were characterized by a sort of calloused, calculating knowing and beset by quarrelsome impatience. The little ones, who had no claim to power, leverage, or virtue, who were continually vulnerable, were also the ones able to hope and dream of better futures. In time they were to experience the future of their dreams. It was the small and powerless ones who received the promise, who entered the promised land. It is always the way. My vision is that our children will sing the songs of the new Dreaming that will make our places and nations anew. Yet this can be so only if we play our small part. We must tell them the old stories, sing them the old songs, both the songs of our own people and our own faith and the songs and stories of those other peoples with whom we share these continents. If we can be faithful in this small thing, we can rest at the end of day sure that hope and faith need not die on this threatened land.

NOTES

1. FROM THE SECULAR CITY TO A THEOLOGY OF THE LAND

1. R. G. Stringer, "Noonkanbah Reflections," *Trinity Occasional Papers,* 2 (Jan. 1983): 3-12.
2. For example, Gibson Winter outlines such a dispute in the Mackenzie River Valley in northern Canada. *Liberating Creation: Foundations of Religious Social Ethics* (New York: Crossroad, 1981), pp. 94-105.
3. See for example the claims of Lynn White, discussed below. For the mythological foundation of development thought see Lenore Layman, "Development Ideology in Western Australia, 1933-1965," *Historical Studies* 20 (Oct. 1982): 234-59.
4. *Dayton Daily News,* Nov. 4, 1986, p. 11.
5. *Engage/Social Action* (June 1985): 38.
6. Shantilal P. Bhagat, *The Family Farm: Can It Be Saved?* (Elgin, Ill.: Brethren Press, 1985), p. 19.
7. Lorette Picciano-Hanson, "Can We Afford to Let the Cockeyed System of Farm and Tax Policies Continue?" *Engage/Social Action* (June 1985): 36.
8. William Sloane Coffin, "Sanctuary for Refugees—and Ourselves," *Christianity and Crisis* 45 (Mar. 18, 1984): 75, 76.
9. "Black Australia in the Seventies," speech given at the Australian National University.
10. L. Brown and E. Wolf, *Soil Erosion,* Worldwatch Paper 60 (Washington: Worldwatch Institute, 1984).

11. Brian Roberts, *Land Ethics—a Necessary Addition to Australian Values* (Canberra: Australian National University, 1984), pp. 3, 4; Dean Graetz, "Heartlands," First Series, Australian Broadcasting Commission, 1983.
12. Nancy Bushwick, "Land and Conservation," *Engage/Social Action* (June 1985): 26-33.
13. John Hart, *The Spirit of the Earth: A Theology of the Land* (New York: Paulist Press, 1985), p. 9.
14. *The Changing World Food Prospect: The Nineties and Beyond,* Worldwatch Paper 85 (Washington: Worldwatch Institute, 1988), p. 21.
15. Harvey Cox, *The Secular City: Secularization and Urbanization in Theological Perspective,* rev. ed. (New York: Macmillan, 1966), p. 21.
16. Ibid., p. 24.
17. Lynn White, Jr., "The Historical Roots of Our Ecological Crisis," *Science* 155.37 (1967): 1203-7.
18. Graetz, "Heartlands."
19. Walter Brueggemann, *The Land: Place as Gift, Promise, and Challenge in Biblical Faith* (Philadelphia: Fortress, 1977), p. 3.
20. Ibid., p. 5.
21. Ibid.
22. Anne Buttimer, "Home, Reach, and the Sense of Place," in *The Human Experience of Space and Place,* ed. Anne Buttimer and David Seamon (London: Croom Helm, 1980), p. 167.
23. Ibid., p. 188, n. 10.
24. I refer to the complex of issues relating to distribution, use, ecology, and the global crisis in the rural sector as the crises of "the land" as a matter of style and convenience and not because I intended to exclude issues of the sea and atmosphere.
25. Cox has acknowledged the need for a revision of the simple evolutionary schema of *The Secular City* in later works, such as *The Seduction of the Spirit: The Use and Misuse of People's Religion* (New York: Simon and Schuster, 1973), pp. 56ff.
26. Walter Brueggemann, "The Earth Is the Lord's: A Theology of Earth and Land," *Sojourners* 15, no. 9 (Oct. 1986): 28ff.

2. THE CENTRALITY OF LAND IN ABORIGINAL AND HEBREW RELIGION

1. Rev. Djiniyini, Badaltja, and RRurrambu, quoted in *My Mother the Land,* ed. Ian R. Yule (Galiwin'ku: Galiwin'ku Literature Production Centre, 1980), pp. 8, 33, 10.

2. Quoted in *Religion in Aboriginal Australia: An Anthology,* ed. Max Charlesworth, Howard Murphy, Diane Bell, and Kenneth Maddock (St. Lucia: University of Queensland Press, 1984), p. 7.
3. Mircea Eliade, *The Sacred and the Profane: The Nature of Religion,* trans. by Willard R. Trask (New York: Harcourt, Brace, 1959), pp. 20-65.
4. Ainsle Roberts and Charles Mountford, *The Dreamtime Book: Australian Aboriginal Myths in Paintings and Text* (Adelaide: Rigby, 1973).
5. Charlesworth, *Religion in Aboriginal Australia,* pp. 9, 10.
6. A. E. Newsome, "The Ecomythology of the Red Kangaroo in Central Australia," *Mankind* 12 (1981): 327-33.
7. David Lewis, "The Way of the Nomad," in *From Earlier Fleets: Hemisphere—An Aboriginal Anthology* (Melbourne: Australian Government Publishing Service, 1978) pp. 77-83.
8. Amos Rapoport, "Australian Aborigines and the Definition of Place," *Shelter, Sign and Symbol,* ed. Paul Oliver (London: Barrie and Jenkins, 1975), pp. 41-42.
9. Ronald M. Berndt, *Australian Aboriginal Religion* (Leiden: Brill, 1974), p. 10.
10. Ibid., p. 15.
11. Ibid., pp. 19-20.
12. Walter Brueggemann, *The Land: Place as Gift, Promise, and Challenge in Biblical Faith* (Philadelphia: Fortress, 1977), p. 3.
13. See Judith Wright, "At Cooloola," *The Double Tree: Selected Poems 1942–1976* (Boston: Houghton Mifflin, 1978), pp. 65-66. The poem will be discussed in chapter 6.
14. As C. Dean Freudenberger persuasively argues in "Implications of a New Land Ethic," in *Theology of the Land,* ed. Bernard F. Evans and Gregory D. Cusack (Collegeville, Minn.:" Liturgical Press, 1987), pp. 69-84.
15. Wendell Berry, "Poetry and Place," *Standing by Words* (San Francisco: North Point Press, 1983), pp. 92-199.
16. Robin Attfield, "Christian Attitudes to Nature," *Journal of the History of Ideas* 44 (1983): 374-75.
17. Brueggemann, *The Land,* p. 132.
18. Ibid., pp. 144-45.
19. W. D. Davies, *The Gospel and the Land: Early Christianity and Jewish Territorial Doctrine* (Berkeley: University of California Press, 1974), p. 366.

3. SHATTERING THE TERRITORIAL CHRYSALIS

1. H. Paul Santmire, *The Travail of Nature: The Ambiguous Ecological Promise of Christian Theology* (Philadelphia: Fortress, 1985).

2. W. D. Davies, *The Territorial Dimension of Judaism* (Berkeley: University of California Press, 1981), p. 33.
3. Elias Bickerman, *From Ezra to the Last of the Maccabees: Foundations of Postbiblical Judaism* (New York: Schocken, 1962), p. 45.
4. Ibid., pp. 35-39.
5. J. Christian Beker, *Paul the Apostle* (Philadelphia: Fortress, 1980), pp. 135-38.
6. This is the proper place for the study of the theology of creation; see chapter 1, sec. 4. "Toward a Theology of the Land."
7. Davies, *The Territorial Dimension of Judaism,* pp. 31ff.
8. Ernst Kasemann, "An Apologia for Primitive Christian Eschatology," *Essays on New Testament Themes* (London: SCM Press, 1964), pp. 169-95.
9. W. D. Davies, *The Gospel and the Land: Early Christianity and Jewish Territorial Doctrine* (Berkeley: University of California Press, 1974), p. 375.
10. Walter Brueggemann, *The Land: Place as Gift, Promise, and Challenge in Biblical Faith* (Philadelphia: Fortress, 1977), p. 179.
11. Davies, *The Gospel and the Land,* p. 366.
12. Ibid, p. 368.
13. Davies, *The Territorial Dimension of Judaism,* p. 76.
14. Baruch M. Bokser, "Approaching Sacred Space," *Harvard Theological Review* 78 (1985): 279-99.

4. THE POETICS OF SPACE: PLACE AND SPACE IN THE WESTERN TRADITION

1. Salomon Bochner, "Space," *Dictionary of the History of Ideas* (New York: Charles Scribner's Sons, 1973), pp. 295-307.
2. Salomon Bochner, *The Role of Mathematics in the Rise of Science* (Princeton, N.J.: Princeton University Press, 1966), pp. 152-56.
3. "Space," *The Encyclopedia of Philosophy* (New York: Macmillan, 1967).
4. J. J. C. Smart points out, however, that Newton's dynamics really did not require the metaphysical claim to the absolute existence of space, but could function quite adequately with an inertial system.
5. Compare the views of Lynn White, discussed in chapter 1.
6. David Bohm, *Wholeness and the Implicate Order* (London: Routledge & Kegan Paul, 1980), p. 9.
7. Anne Buttimer, "Home, Reach and the Sense of Place," in *The Human Experience of Space and Place,* ed. Anne Buttimer and David Seamon (London: Croom Helm, 1980), pp. 166-87.

8. Ibid., p. 174.
9. Ibid., p. 186.
10. Gaston Bachelard, *The Poetics of Space,* trans. by Maria Jolas (Boston: Beacon Press, 1969), p. 219.
11. Carle L. Raschke, "The End of Theology," *Journal of the American Academy of Religion* 46 (1978): 159-79. Nathan A. Scott, Jr., "Heidegger's Vision of Poetry as Ontology," *The Poetics of Belief* (Chapel Hill: University of North Carolina Press, 1985), pp. 146-68.
12. It seems that Liberty Hyde Bailey has something similar in mind with his discussion of the importance of backgrounds in shaping a truly human, moral being. *The Holy Earth* (Columbus, Ohio: The National United Methodist Rural Fellowship, 1988).
13. I restrict attention here to the poetic image. It seems that what is said of the poetic image could also be said of the visual image, and perhaps in other ways of musical images.
14. C. S. Song, *Theology from the Womb of Asia* (Maryknoll, N.Y.: Orbis, 1986), pp. 92-93.
15. Ibid., p. 54.
16. Ibid., p. 44.
17. Ibid.
18. Wendell Berry, *The Unsettling of America* (San Francisco: Sierra Club Books, 1977), pp. 27-29.

5. THE CHRISTIFICATION OF HOLY SPACE: INCARNATION AND THE LAND

1. H. Paul Santmire, *The Travail of Nature: The Ambiguous Ecological Promise of Christian Theology* (Philadelphia: Fortress, 1985) p. 6.
2. "Land, Theology, and the Future," in *Theology of the Land,* ed. Leonard Weber et al. (Collegeville, Minn.: Liturgical Press, 1987), pp. 85-87.
3. W. D. Davies, *The Gospel and the Land: Early Christianity and Jewish Territorial Doctrine* (Berkeley: University of California Press, 1974), pp. 352, 365.
4. C. S. Song, *Theology from the Womb of Asia* (Maryknoll, N.Y.: Orbis, 1986), p. 56.
5. Bernard Brandon Scott, *Jesus, Symbol-Maker for the Kingdom* (Philadelphia: Fortress, 1981), pp. 1-4.
6. Gaston Bachelard, *The Poetics of Space* (Boston: Beacon Press, 1969), pp. 4, 6.
7. Davies, *The Gospel and the Land,* p. 366.
8. Eduard Schillebeeckx, *Jesus: An Experiment in Christology,* trans. by Hubert Hoskins (New York: Crossroad, 1986), p. 200.

9. Ibid., p. 219.
10. Davies, *The Gospel and the Land*, p. 352.
11. John Cobb, *God and the World* (Philadelphia: Westminster, 1969); Grace Jantzen, *God's World, God's Body* (Westminster, 1984).
12. Thomas F. Torrance, *Space, Time and Incarnation* (London: Oxford University Press, 1969), p. 67.
13. Ibid.
14. Ibid., pp. 75, 78.

6. DEFINING INCARNATIONAL PRAXIS

1. Wendell Berry, *Sabbaths* (San Francisco: North Point Press, 1987), p. 17.
2. Judith Wright, *The Double Tree: Selected Poems 1942-1976* (Boston: Houghton Mifflin, 1978) pp. 65-66.
3. Ibid., p. 126.
4. Kath Walker, *My People: A Kath Walker Collection* (Milton, Queensland: Jacaranda Press, 1970), p. 94. (Since publication of this book, Kath Walker has adopted the name Oodgeroo of the tribe Noonuccal.)
5. Bruce Chatwin, *The Songlines* (New York: Viking, 1987).
6. Comments in private correspondence with the author.
7. Marion Shoard, *This Land Is Our Land: The Struggle for Britain's Countryside* (London: Paladin Grafton, 1987), uses the aesthetic notion of landscape to fashion an analysis of environmental problems in the United Kingdom and to formulate a proposal for their resolution.
8. Ronald M. Berndt, *An Adjustment Movement in Arnhem Land* (Paris: Mouton, 1962); Peter Willis, *Riders in the Chariot: Aboriginal Conversion to Christianity in Remote Australia* (Canberra: Charles Strong Memorial Trust, 1987).
9. Wendell Berry, *The Unsettling of America* (San Francisco: Sierra Club Books, 1977). See especially ch. 2, "The Ecological Crisis as a Crisis of Character," and ch. 4, "The Agricultural Crisis and a Crisis of Culture."
10. Don Rogers, "He Decided to Plant," *United Theological Seminary Bulletin: Journal of Theology* (Mar. 1985): 37-39.
11. Wendell Berry, *Home Economics* (San Francisco: North Point Press, 1987), p. 146.
12. *The Land Report* offers regular reports on research findings and the work of this institute. Available from the Land Institute, 2440 E. Water Well Road, Salina, Kan. 67401.